'O'Brien's beautiful memoir *Bush School* takes us back to a time when students said 'good-oh' and teachers were well-respected within their communities. We watch as O'Brien becomes a teacher; placing the children and their learning at the centre of his work whilst courageously navigating the isolated life of a remote town during the early sixties. O'Brien's story is told with great integrity. He explores the unique challenges and opportunities faced by small schools as well as delving into the grand endeavour that is "teaching". *Bush School* reminds us that teaching is an act of service and that teachers—then and now—are indispensable.'

—Gabbie Stroud, author of *Teacher*

'So many wonderful books, plays and films centre upon the importance of a dedicated and inspiring teacher in the lives of the very young. The reason is simple. Such teachers, and they are indeed rare, have a lifetime influence upon their pupils. I believe Peter O'Brien is such a teacher. Given *Bush School* chronicles the earliest days of Peter's teaching career, it's also interesting to note his memoir has "a coming of age" aspect. A coming of age for Peter himself as he discovers so much about who he is in the remote community to which he's been assigned. Delightfully composed, *Bush School* has many voices. There is the evocation of a bygone era; there is historical and sociological comment; there is a strong sense of humanity; and above all, there is charm and warmth on every page.'

—Judy Nunn, author of *Khaki Town*

Bush School

PETER O'BRIEN

A 20-year-old teacher fresh out of college.
A tiny one-teacher school in a paddock miles from anywhere.
Eighteen children aged between 5 and 15. Nothing to it!

ALLEN&UNWIN
SYDNEY·MELBOURNE·AUCKLAND·LONDON

Allen & Unwin
83 Alexander Street
Crows Nest NSW 2065
Australia
Phone: (61 2) 8425 0100
Email: info@allenandunwin.com
Web: www.allenandunwin.com

 A catalogue record for this
book is available from the
National Library of Australia

ISBN 978 1 76106 702 0

Maps by Mika Tabata
Internal design by Bookhouse
Set in Bembo MT Pro by Bookhouse, Sydney
Printed in Australia by McPherson's Printing Group

10 9 8 7 6 5 4 3 2 1

 The paper in this book is FSC® certified.
FSC® promotes environmentally responsible,
socially beneficial and economically viable
management of the world's forests.

*For the children of the Bush School,
all my Balmain Teachers' College peers,
Patricia and Sean*

⌒

Bush School is a memoir and the people, places and events recounted in it are all from sixty years ago. It is the result of the author's memory of that long-gone past and, as with all memoirs, it may not reflect the way others remember those times and places. All names have been changed to protect the privacy of the individuals.

WEABONGA DISTRICT

WALCHA

Limbri

TAMWORTH

Nemingha

WEABONGA

Ingelba

Dungowan

Niangala

Ogunbil

Bowling
Alley Point

Nundle

To Nowendoc

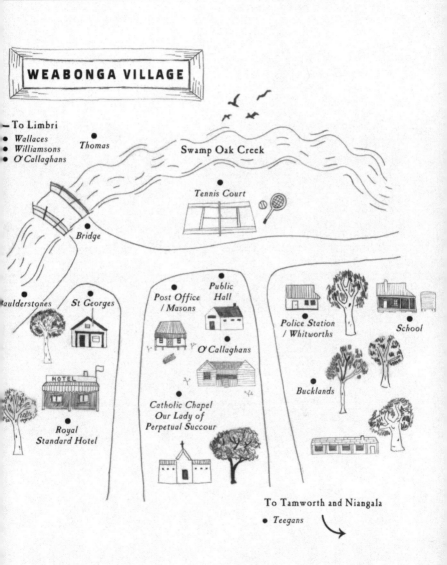

WEABONGA VILLAGE

To Limbri
- Wallaces
- Williamsons
- O'Callaghans

Thomas

Swamp Oak Creek

Tennis Court

Bridge

Baulderstones

St Georges

HOTEL

Royal
Standard Hotel

Post Office
/ Masons

Public
Hall

O'Callaghans

Catholic Chapel
Our Lady of
Perpetual Succour

Police Station
/ Whitworths

School

Bucklands

To Tamworth and Niangala
- Teegans

People of the Story

School people

The Baulderstone family: Will in Grade Four and Gary in Grade
Three. They had a dad, Max, and a mum, June. The family
lived on the edge of the village in the old Baulderstone
family home, inherited by Max.

The Deer family: Mary in Kindergarten. They had a dad,
Frank, and a mum, Rose, plus several younger daughters.
The family lived on a cattle and sheep property about seven
miles out of the village on the road to Dungowan.

Allan Flood: the Inspector of Schools for the Armidale Region.

The Mason family: Jack in Grade Five and Steve in Grade
Two. They came from a village home, which had the post
office on a section of glassed-in veranda. They had a single
mum, Sue, and a grandfather, Tim Bourke, whose home it
was and who resided with them. Jack and Steve's dad had

separated from their mum and was living elsewhere; he did not come to see his children.

The Mount family: Merrilyn in Kindergarten. She had a dad, Merv, and a mum, Heather. They lived in a habitable section of the old Royal Standard Hotel in the village.

The O'Callaghan family: Tom in Grade Eight and Debbie in Grade Five. They came from a sheep property just out of the village on the Limbri Road. They had a single dad—a widower, Cyril—and a large extended family.

The O'Callaghan family: Mike in Grade Four, Phil in Grade Three and Charlie in Grade One. They had a dad, Lawrie, and a mum, Jill. The family lived in the village.

Note that the two O'Callaghan families were related. Lawrie was the eldest son of Cyril O'Callaghan, so Lawrie was the oldest of Tom and Debbie's many brothers, and Tom and Debbie were the aunt and uncle to Lawrie's boys Mike, Phil and Charlie.

The Teegan family: Lindie in Grade Five and Susie in Grade Two. They came from a sheep property some ten miles out of the village on the back road to Ingelba. They had a dad, Vic, and a mum, Jan. Their older sister, Wendy, was away at boarding school.

The Thomas family: Vickie in Grade Five, Mark in Grade Four and Carol in Grade Two. They had a dad, Dan, and a mum, Molly, and the family lived in a village home.

The Wallace family: Joe in Grade Four and Jimmy in Grade One. They had a dad, Tony, and a mum, Marie. The family lived on a sheep-grazing property about ten miles from the village along the Limbri Road and beyond the Williamsons' property.

The Whitworth Family: Sandra in Grade 5, Rick in Grade Four and Robbie in Grade Three. They a dad, Bill, and a mum, Monica, and the family lived in the village in the old police station.

Others

The Bucklands: Perc and his sister Ethel, septuagenarian pensioners. They lived in a compound of three huts on a village site of about two acres, overlooking the school.

Bon Knox: Bon was the mail-car contractor who delivered post and small items from Tamworth to the village every Friday. He also ran a carriage service so provided transport, for a fee, to anyone needing to travel along his mail route.

The Watermains: Allan and Claudine lived on their grazing property on the Limbri Road about seven miles past Barry White's place and nine miles or so beyond the Williamsons' homestead. Allan and Claudine had no children.

Barry White: a local grazier on the Limbri Road, a few miles beyond the Williamsons. He had never married.

The Williamson family: George, an elderly widower dad; his four adult daughters, Barbara, Elizabeth, Margaret and Joan; and his adult son, Paul. The Williamsons ran a sheep property some three miles from the village along the Limbri Road. George and Paul lived on the property at all times, and occasionally one of the adult daughters also lived at home to assist in caring for their dad.

1

'Here we go,' I said to myself. 'Can I do this?' The hardest test of my short life was about to hit me. 'Lord, I hope it's calm, that we all survive and there's a soft landing.'

At last the academic year was to begin, a week later than normal. On this first day, I had arrived very early at the little bush school. By just after seven o'clock I had opened up and, not knowing for certain what to prepare on our blackboard, had created a simple chalk picture of this tiny, remote village, Weabonga, with its one-room school on a rise in the centre. By laying chalk sticks on their side, I'd produced wide sweeps of colour in each stroke. Children were pictured playing in the yard, and a teacher was leaning over the veranda rail, apparently welcoming them. I was hoping this vivid board would encourage the children to talk easily together and interact confidently with me.

At around eight-thirty parents began arriving, accompanied by subdued kids. I took details for each student, adding them to the official roll. Needing to know as much as I could, I gathered facts about every child. In Armidale my inspector would be waiting for me to call with student numbers, hoping I would vindicate his decision to appoint me in charge and allow a reopening of the school a week late.

Pupils from eight families had come to enrol: at least two from each home, while some families enrolled three. Eighteen pupils, thirteen boys and five girls in six grades: now I knew what I faced. Our oldest was a thirteen-year-old lad—'nearly fourteen, Sir'—and the youngest a five-year-old boy. Much kinship was reported: sets of brothers, a set of sisters, and two brother–sister groups. There were cousins and an aunt and uncle. Twelve of the kids came from five homes in the village and six from properties outside its borders. No child had to travel more than ten miles, but the two families furthest from the school would have to transport their children to and fro each day; all the others could walk easily enough.

When the parents left, saying their goodbyes, I stood on the veranda ready to invite the children to join me in the schoolroom. But, where were they? Not one was anywhere near the entryway. As I searched for the children, the words of an aged, farm-reared aunt came to mind. Upon hearing of my appointment to a remote country school, she had given some spontaneous advice. 'Bush children run and hide at the sight of strangers. Give them time and be gentle. You'll do all right if you keep that in mind. Never rush them.' This had made me smile, although I had accepted that the words were probably wise.

The children were scattered about the yard and well towards the fences. Boys were with boys under the four huge pines on the furthest boundary, and girls with girls down near the school gate, below the path and its long lines of clipped privet hedge on either side. Not wanting to shout the first words they would hear from me—*gentle, be gentle*—I walked nearer to each group and quietly asked them to join me inside. Then I sat at my desk and waited.

The oldest lad, the thirteen-year-old, came in first a few minutes later. 'Tom,' he said as he walked in determinedly. He struck me as relatively mature, solid and sensible, and he talked with me in a quiet but confident manner. I didn't want to rush to judgement but I was really pleased with this first meeting. We discussed his family and the schoolwork for which he might need my assistance. Being a post-primary student, he would be doing his lessons by correspondence.

Tom's sister, Debbie, a few years younger, was next to join us. A little more diffident than Tom, she seemed a sturdy, sensible girl and said she was in Grade Five.

Soon after, Vickie and Lindie, about the same age as Debbie, sidled in. Holding hands, they smiled a little; whether that was to break any tension they were feeling or simply through shyness, I wasn't concerned—I was just happy they were smiling.

Then two younger girls hopped up the stairs and skipped into the room. I read their smiles as genuine, a breakout of a delight to be here. I smiled back, hoping to reinforce their interest in school. By now I was losing track of names. Of course, they'd been listed in the register with their parents' help, and I decided I'd worry about them a little later by preparing a small cheat

3

sheet to which I could refer if memory failed. For now, I just wanted the kids to feel welcome and of interest to me.

The six children in the room commenced chatting, tentatively but with an increasing ease. After another ten minutes or so, all twelve younger boys arrived in one group—perhaps they'd given each other courage. They pushed forward and rolled into the room as an entangled ball, with arms around each other's shoulders in solidarity.

Now all the children were here, they sat comfortably as one group, regardless of age. They chose where to sit, on the floor or on chairs, and chatted freely. I indicated I'd like to know about their lives, their families, their pets, their favourite things—indeed, about anything and everything of importance to them. I asked them to use their first names when commencing to speak. 'I really want to get to know you well, and I'll need your help at first with names. Is that all right?'

Nods came from all around the room, so we began our conversation.

Tom, the teenager, reported, 'I spent most of December and January helping two of my older brothers fence around our biggest paddock. It's always called Finn's paddock, about five hundred acres all up. The ute couldn't be driven right around it 'cause it's real hilly and rocky, so we had to cart a big lot of wire and posts in by hand. It was as hard as billyo and as hot as Hades but we just got on with it and helped each other. Me brothers taught me lots about fencing. It was beaut.'

Will, one of the younger boys, started off with another story. 'Yeah, when it got real hot in December we talked our dads into building us a bit of a dam on the creek. A bit of a swimming hole for us kids.'

Rick added, 'It took a few days of asking and reminding, and finally our dads said for us to stop badgering them and they might do it.'

Gary called out, 'We all shouted, "Hooray, you beauty!"'

Will came back in with, 'Our dads said, "Righty-ho. We'll give it a go."'

'So some families got together and worked out what to do.'

'Mr Baulderstone, Will's dad, said to find a spot where a tree had already come down from a flood, so we picked just the place on the creek below Mark's house.'

'By jings it was fun. We got lots of rocks from around the creek and piled them at the end of the little waterhole against the tree stump.'

It became clear that most of the children, at least all those from the village, had been involved in this community project, and many had something to say.

'It took us a couple of days. We had to take a spell every now and then but.'

And Jack called out, 'We didn't do too bad. Within half a mo' of putting the first rocks in place water started to back up.'

Another reported, 'Mike and me tried to carry a real big rock. We almost went cross-eyed, and our dads told us not to be such mutton-heads. They said to let them finish it off. They showed us what to do but, and with all of us trying we dropped it in the best spot.'

'We made a sort of fence in the water against the rocks. Mr Mason said it was a palishade or somethin'. It looked good-oh,' was a small boy's contribution.

They went on, all eager now to be involved but still mindful of taking turns.

'Our dads took a smoko every little bit, and it seemed to take a terrible lot of time. But we had a good pool after a couple a' days.'

'When it was ready enough the dads said it'd do. They told us never to be dumb clucks around water, never to be silly coots.'

'All the pops said we had to be real careful around the creek. They said if they found us playing up and being silly near the water they'd tan our hides for us, and stop the swimmin'.'

'Mr Whitworth said we mustn't chuck away our chance for fun by doin' anything dangerous. We knew what he meant so.'

'All holidays we mucked about around the pool and made up heaps of games and competitions. Rick could stay under longer than anyone.'

'Jack was first to swim sort of properly, and he made up a mad game where he picked us into water polo teams. Jack said it was just like the Melbourne Olympics. We all said he was a bit of a silly-billy. We all joined in but.'

A smaller girl—Carol, I remembered—spoke up for the first time. 'My mum thanked all the dads who helped. Mum said the men had been nice to the kids.'

We also heard of some individual activities.

Vickie, one of the three older girls, reported, 'My mum and me made many candles. Mum showed me how to melt down mutton fat. We added a string for a wick and nice-smelling

6

things so when the candle burnt it had a sweet perfume. My mum and me went through the bush behind our house and gathered lemon myrtle leaves to boil up for their oils to scent our candles.'

Her brother, Mark, added, 'I never noticed any smells, but the candles lit up the house nice and lively at night.'

We heard of lads who'd been taught how to safely set a rabbit trap; of lasses who'd commenced to use dress patterns for sewing their own clothes; of boys who spent lots of time each day working with and helping their dads; of girls who were encouraged to join with their mums in cooking for the family. The kids told of caring for poddies, of digging and weeding in the family gardens, of feeding and looking after chooks.

They didn't gush: everything was said with care and thought, and a sense that they took my invitation to chat responsibly. They were slow, but never ponderous and never staid—there was a liveliness and vitality about them all. They were respectful to each other, all listening quietly as the others spoke. Any statement from one would prompt lines from the others. And they were just as respectful to me. I had invited them; they would respond seriously and treat my request sensibly.

This all gave me a different feeling to what I'd experienced with the boys and girls at Kegworth Public School in Leichhardt, Sydney, my only previous school, where I had spent my first two years as a teacher. Those city kids had been quick-witted, intending to entertain as much as to explain, while these Weabonga children were guileless, with an appealing innocence, their openness and honesty a little disarming. At Kegworth, the children had told me much but wrapped the important revelations in a tall tale or distraction. Here, I heard of life exactly as it was; there was no attempt to paper over reality.

As I listened, a memory came to me of talking with several mums at the Kegworth school gate after the final bell. We'd made a pact that I would believe about a third of what I heard from the children about life at home, while the mothers would believe about the same fraction when the children talked about school. That rule couldn't apply here in Weabonga, where I detected nothing but unvarnished truth from the eighteen pupils yarning with me. I did find the openness that first day unexpected and very appealing.

2

My career route to appointment as teacher-in-charge at Weabonga had been straightforward, following a long-established trajectory for male teachers. After spending 1956 and '57 in training at Balmain Teachers' College, I'd received my first appointment.

When the department's official letter arrived in mid-January 1958, my anxiety soared. Not having heard of Kegworth, I assumed it to be a one-teacher country school. I felt strongly that I was quite unprepared to take on such a challenge, having never taught a Kindergarten, Grade One or Grade Two class. I felt a real lack of knowledge and expertise in assisting beginner readers, which I would surely need in a small country school, and I wasn't sure if I could lead, manage and teach the mixture of ages and grades that I might find there. I was too raw, too inexperienced and too likely to get things wrong—and the country pupils and families couldn't regain a lost year if I proved inept. I just wasn't ready for the responsibility.

When I contacted the Department of Education to learn the location, I was told, 'Kegworth is easy to find, just a few hundred yards off Parramatta Road in Leichhardt.'

'Really, it's in Sydney?'

'Sure is. How lucky are you? Could've been Woop Woop on your first appointment.'

My experiences in those first two years of teaching were to bear out the saying 'Be careful what you wish for.'

Kegworth had many drawbacks—poor supervision, poor leadership models, little professional stimulus or discussion, and no assistance with educational or schooling matters—but I developed in many important ways. I found I was able to work easily with children, and that they were cooperative and seemed to enjoy working with me. I came to understand the importance for my own teaching of thorough preparation. I learnt that kids love creative activities. In taking charge of the school sport and music programs, I came to know the hundred or more primary kids, and I enjoyed that aspect of the role.

I was soon pleased to speak with Kegworth parents about their children, and I felt I could do so as a professional, explaining the class programs, the educational aims for their child and how the youngster was progressing. I felt comfortable suggesting what the parents might do to support their child's educational development. I looked forward to working more closely with parents in future appointments.

Kegworth allowed me to form a good idea of what I wanted to achieve in my career. And although still lacking certainty, I came to believe I'd be able to assist and lead any primary class I was asked to teach.

Because of the bonding arrangements that young student teachers signed to receive financial support in our training, we were required to spend at least two years in a country school at some time in our careers. So I wasn't surprised when, towards the end of my second year as a teacher, I received a departmental posting as teacher-in-charge of Guy Fawkes Primary School, a one-teacher school in the New England area of New South Wales. I knew I still had a lot to learn, but I believed I could now handle a small bush school.

Much of my new-found confidence was due to the nature of the Kegworth kids. I was going to miss them. As a group, they were chirpy and funny; they tried jokes and quips, and laughed vigorously at any attempts at humour from fellow students or from me. They were extremely amenable and would happily engage with me in whatever learning activity I offered them.

Those cheerful city kids had allowed me glimpses of alternative approaches to teaching. I'd noted their excitement and heightened engagement when we were able to include ideas and topics they'd suggested, so I'd determined to expand children's decision-making in my next school.

Our year ended with the annual school concert at Leichhardt Town Hall for which I'd prepared the primary combined choir to sing 'The Little Drummer Boy'. Both the pupils and their parents loved the song, and I was proud of the children and pleased for their success.

I wasn't on fire about the Guy Fawkes appointment. While teaching at Kegworth I had remained living with my parents, so the sudden shift to the remote countryside was a wrench, even though by then I was more than ready to move out of the family home. Another reason for my reluctance to leave was the friendship I'd formed with a delightful young lady, Patricia—I would certainly miss her.

Patricia had impressed me powerfully when she'd accepted my invitation to the Kegworth school's concert. I was intrigued that a young, single woman had chosen to come along with me, having no other connection to the event. I was charmed when she told me how much she'd enjoyed the carols from the choir.

Our friendship had come about in a meeting at Surryville, a large public dance hall on City Road. At such events the ritual of the last dance was well understood. During the evening, a young man would ask one of his dance partners for the final dance of the night, booking this in advance. If the young lady accepted, both knew she was also accepting that the man would accompany her home. From such beginnings, longer-term friendships could bloom.

One evening I had escorted Patricia to her home, chatting on the way. She was charming, witty, easy to talk to and quite a beauty—I had struck the last-dance jackpot. As we'd said goodbye at her front door, we had arranged to see each other again a week or so later. Having enjoyed that outing, we commenced meeting up once a fortnight or so.

To take up my appointment at Guy Fawkes in January 1960, I had to rely on public transport, the norm for most young teachers taking up country appointments. A few days before the start of term one, I travelled on the Brisbane Mail, an overnight train from Sydney, alighting at Armidale early the next morning. An all-day journey in the mail car east from the Armidale Post Office delivered me to Guy Fawkes, on top of the Great Dividing Range.

The village was situated in visually stunning country. Traffic passed regularly through Guy Fawkes along the main road down to Grafton, so although distant from Sydney it didn't feel too isolated. As a site to begin my country schoolmaster career, it looked full of promise. I was struck by the friendliness of the family with whom I was to live and enjoyed the comforts of their well-furnished and properly equipped homestead.

So, I was disappointed when only six children turned up for enrolment. I told the small band of presenting parents that I'd need to speak with my inspector and take his direction. When I rang, he ordered me to return to Armidale as soon as practicable.

My very brief meeting with the Guy Fawkes families had set firmly in my mind that school education was extremely important in a small rural setting. Until then, I'd had next to no appreciation of the importance of bush schools. The bush wasn't alien to me: I had holidayed for short periods as a boy at Dunedoo and Tenterfield, and as teenager at Miandetta, outside Nyngan. Like many city youngsters at the time, I had access through my family to country properties of relatives and friends. But I hadn't spent any time learning about the realities of remote country communities. Now, as a city boy rapidly turning into a country teacher, I made my way back into town thinking deeply about the vital role of one-teacher schooling for children and their families. I was ready to give it my best shot—but where was this shot to be fired?

I'd expected the Inspector, Mr Flood, to be an old fuddy-duddy, so I was surprised to find him a warm, pleasant and supportive chap, aged in his mid-forties. However, I was still in awe of this august person who held the power to sustain or restrain my hoped-for career. Fortunately he was caring and respectful. I listened intently as he outlined the educational needs of the communities in his inspectorate. He asked that I consider three locations, all needing an immediate teacher-in-charge appointment: Wards Mistake, a second location that I don't remember, and Weabonga. Where I would like to teach?

About Weabonga, he said, 'This is a location much in my mind. It's my most remote school, and the local people have been very actively advocating for a teaching appointment.' He added, 'I agree with them—of course their school should be reopened. All children, especially the most isolated, deserve an opportunity for schooling. But my hands have been tied. I had no teacher to send until you turned up so fortuitously.'

He told me more about the Weabonga kids. 'The school has been closed at times because of the difficulty in staffing. There have been several interruptions. Continuity in schooling for the Weabonga children has been hampered by teachers resigning after only a short time. In addition, my last few visits have me concerned about the children's progress, and I'm keen to place a teacher there who'll stay for a reasonable period and gradually return their achievements to reasonable levels. I do worry about Weabonga.'

What I knew of Wards Mistake was that it took its name from a notorious nineteenth-century bushranger who'd roamed the countryside under the pseudonym of Captain Thunderbolt. I surely wasn't going to repeat this mistake, so that town was dismissed.

The second school must have seemed bland and unexciting, as I've never been able to recall its name.

Then I turned to the third. My assessment of Weabonga was that it really needed a missionary rather than a teacher. But it was quite clear which option Mr Flood wished me to accept, so my response was partly formulated to gain his appreciation. Perhaps this was a bit cringingly obsequious, but I was young enough to think the most appropriate reaction was to agree with an authority figure and to sublimate my sense of what was best for me.

'I'm happy to teach at any one of them but would like to go where I'm most needed.'

His relief was obvious: Weabonga it was.

That day we parted as a very pleased inspector and, I thought, a young teacher perhaps owed something for his amenability.

⌣

I stayed the night in an Armidale boarding house with a friend from my National Service days in the Sydney University Regiment, and it was a relief to spend time with him. This brief respite helped me get ready to move on to Weabonga.

As I fell asleep my mind ranged over many matters, including some consideration of Patricia. Her grandfather, with whom she lived, considered himself responsible for her welfare and took this role very seriously. When I'd commenced taking her on outings, Grandfather had insisted on meeting me.

His second question was, 'What's your employment, young man?'

'I'm a schoolteacher,' I replied, and immediately he appeared more welcoming.

'Well, that's good,' he said. 'And where might you take Patricia when you go out?'

I weighed my response. 'Probably the Ashfield CYO Saturday dance at the town hall.'

This mention of the Catholic Youth Organisation had him beaming.

Clearly, young men who didn't pass his assessment couldn't take his granddaughter out a second time.

Grandfather maintained a close interest and patrolled our comings and goings. Whenever I returned my friend to her home, no matter the hour, Grandfather would allow us a short time alone on the veranda. After about ten to fifteen minutes, the front door would open, the outside light come on, and Grandfather would be at the door waiting to make sure Patricia got safely inside. On at least one occasion he called out, 'Time to come in, Miss Muffet.'

It was no wonder that other young men had given up interest in Patricia. When I appeared, the scene was clear. That suited me fine.

Having met the grandparents and having heard something of their history, I admired them both. Grandfather had become secretary to the Bourke branch of the Australian Workers Union just after the turn of the century when he was but sixteen. In 1917 he had stood for election on an anti-conscription platform for Labor in Armidale; he was unsuccessful but by less than a thousand votes in a fiercely conservative seat. Delivery of white feathers to his letterbox by anonymous donors hadn't deterred him, and Grandma had backed him all the way. She had converted to Catholicism to marry him against the wishes of her sternly Presbyterian family, who owned a huge sheep-grazing property near Bourke. And the couple had sent three sons to the Second World War, with one spending years as a prisoner of the Japanese on the Burma Railway, suffering through Hellfire Pass.

In viewing the great love and esteem that my friend had for her grandfather, I was easily reconciled to his way of showing concern for his granddaughter. Grandfather and I had much in common: my own concerns for Patricia's welfare were growing to match his. We were on the same side.

3

Weabonga is only a two-hour drive direct from Armidale, but my trip took me the best part of two days after my meeting with Mr Flood. Travelling from Armidale via the morning train to Tamworth, I waited overnight for a next-day lift with the mail car to Weabonga. I met up with Bon Knox, the mailman and driver, at the Tamworth PO and travelled all that second day with him, chatting about the district and Weabonga. He was a great guide and had relatives in the area, so his local knowledge was useful.

Weabonga is on the western lip of the Great Divide just under the highest country, a little down from the 'tops'. Swamp Oak Creek, which runs through the village, flows down to the Cockburn River, a tributary of the Namoi, then the Darling and, finally, the Murray. So, rain that falls on Weabonga reaches the Southern Ocean more than a thousand miles away. The village is hemmed in on every side by steep hills, with no flat country anywhere around. Everything is pitched at an angle, and there are no grand, sweeping vistas.

Bon and I approached Weabonga heading east from Tamworth through the villages of Nemingha, Dungowan and Ogunbil. Lunch could have been had in Dungowan, at a little riverside hotel, but we pushed on. The road ran alongside the Peel River in many places; there were extensive, rich river flats, and the countryside delighted me—mostly level and gently undulating, with trees distributed here and there as in an arboretum.

However, just after Ogunbil the road began to rise, and we commenced to travel via the Port Stephens Cutting: a long, steep and very narrow stretch from the valley floor to the heights of the Divide. Originally the main northern highway had passed up the Cutting, but it had always been problematic. Bon told me that for years there were gates and gatekeepers at the top and bottom, and traffic was restricted to one-way flows, changing direction every hour or two. When it all became too difficult as traffic increased, the highway was moved to run along the New England Highway route.

We stopped for a late lunch at the Niangala village, and Bon invited me to join him in the wine salon, as there was no pub. A few wine salons were still scattered around the state but had become something of a rarity. The attraction for the Niangala proprietor was the salon's cheapness to run and the low cost of its beverages for the clientele.

It was the first week of February, but Niangala, on top of the mountain range, was quite cool. I accepted a glass of port. There were two chatty locals having a sherry, and they introduced themselves. 'Peter,' I responded and we shook hands.

We'd all returned to contemplating our own glass, when one spoke again. 'Can you fight, Pete? We could have a bit of a go out the back if you want to put up your mitts and give it a try.'

Just a little startled, I feinted to the left. 'Thanks for the invite,' I said, 'but I'd better stay in good shape for when I meet the people in Weabonga.'

Bon and I set off on our final leg back down to the Limbri turn-off. Weabonga was now about ten miles off to the right. Niangala had been fascinating—and somewhat challenging as an introduction to the district where I would spend at least the next two years. As we drove, I wondered about my choices. *What have I landed myself in? If those guys at the wine salon are a sample of the locals, I'm up for a trying few years.*

The country took on a heavily treed aspect, and my sense of remoteness became stronger. An atmosphere of the high country strengthened; just the look of the vegetation and the nature of the bush carried that impression. Weabonga was remote as the Inspector had intimated: twenty-five miles to Walcha, twenty to Limbri (on the main northern railway) and thirty to Tamworth. Connecting these three were gravel roads that rose and fell in constant upheaval, and swept right to left and back again; my experience was of them always being poorly graded. There was no reason to pass through Weabonga, so traffic there was sparse, almost non-existent. I realised on this drive with Bon that I was about to be stranded, dependent on the locals for company, stimulation and friendship—for everything!

Weabonga is at about 2500 feet above sea level, around five hundred feet lower than the peak of the Divide. That first day

I could see it would enjoy a mild climate most of the summer but would get quite cold in winter, with snow at times.

The sun was setting when we drove down into the small valley around Swamp Oak Creek where the village was situated. Bon told of the name, Weabonga. Previously called Rywung, then Swamp Oak, the village later became 'the meeting or resting place between the hills', or Weabonga in the local Aboriginal language, Bon explained. This title seemed appropriate as I took my first glimpses of my new home.

Motoring into the village we passed a tumbledown group of tin huts on the right, a shabby weatherboard house to the left, and a more substantial, well-built but not well-maintained weatherboard cottage with solid brick foundations, again to the right. At a corner, where the main road took a sharp turn left, was a largish, falling-apart tin shed that might have once been a hall and, opposite, a tennis court behind sagging chicken wire. More dwellings were visible in the bush and trees further down the slope, but Bon stopped and explained that I would stay in the shabby house on the left. My hosts were to be the O'Callaghan family.

I observed a cottage constructed of roughly sawn timber that didn't appear to have received any protective paint or treatment in its history. The walls were weathered to a silvery sheen, and the tin roof was rusted and pitted all over, with several sheets lifting from their nails. A small front veranda was nestled between two gable ends, with a couple of tar-paper sheets tacked across the posts. No garden was visible.

It struck me as quite miserable. I hoped that wasn't so.

I was met on the front veranda by the woman of the house, who introduced herself as Jill O'Callaghan. Nothing more. She was quite striking, handsome in a way, but tall and gaunt, dressed in what must have been her everyday clothes, well-worn but clean, drained of any original colour through years of washing, all covered with an apron. She said, 'Just follow me,' and set off into the interior. There were no welcoming words.

'Fine,' I responded, taken somewhat aback, and followed, weighed down by my heavy suitcase. It held enough clothing to carry me over two years, along with a few books I felt were vital for my work. One suitcase to sustain one life: a simple life, indeed, with no great expectations.

Passing through the front door, I lost sight of my landlady. Bright sunlight was instantly replaced by a dense gloom, and before my eyes adjusted I couldn't see. Placing my bag on the floor, I called out for assistance. 'Hello. Hello, Jill? I'm sorry but I can't see anything. Could you help me?'

What a ninny, I thought. *What next? She'll think I'm a total dill.*

While waiting to be rescued I realised this room had no windows, although I gradually made out the dim outlines of three or four doors.

My landlady re-emerged, now carrying a lit pressure lantern. Again she said, 'Follow me,' and showed me to the kitchen, with its family-sized table and the old wood-burning stove that dominated the space. All meals were to be served there. Off the kitchen was a room with a bath and basin; no taps were visible or any means of heating water evident.

We then went back through the front door onto the veranda. Jill showed me an area created by tacking up thin sheets of paper impregnated with a bitumen mixture. Inside this makeshift area, on the rough timber boards, was a bed. She said, 'This is where you'll sleep.'

There were no pegs or nails to hang a hat, no door, no rug for bare feet on cold mornings, no bookshelf for a voracious reader, no bedside cupboard for a lamp or glass of water, no light source—just a bed and a suitcase for the next two years.

I was dumbfounded. I wasn't a spoilt darling and could accept some discomfort, but surely leaving my home and family, being parted from my romantic interest, being deprived of all cultural and social interaction, and being isolated hundreds of miles from all I knew and loved were sufficient sacrifices for the people of New South Wales? So why was I being made to accept these living conditions?

As I sat on the bed, I tried to excuse much of the apparent hardship by thinking of my appointment as a 'grand endeavour'. I felt I had to believe in something transcending the perceived awful reality in order to give the experience some credibility and to increase my forbearance and acceptance.

Jill left me there to 'settle in'. Nothing difficult about that. I just placed my suitcase on the floor.

Eventually she invited me to the table and served an evening meal of baked young rabbit and potatoes with squash: an interesting dinner, not without some flavour. The rabbit was, in fact, quite delicious. Gramma squash was new to me, and I found it bland and unpleasant. I ate alone, as the family had completed their own meal. Some quiet voices had been audible, but I hadn't met the husband or children.

I didn't know it at the time, but that meal established a routine. Thereafter, I was to always eat alone and usually to be served rabbit with squash.

Retreating to bed in my tar-paper cubby, I was in a fairly black and dangerous mood. But thoughts of Patricia calmed me a little.

Early on, perhaps on our fourth night out together, she and I had talked of how we'd met. We discussed the awkwardness associated with getting a conversation going with a stranger at a dance. Both of us were a bit disparaging of the easy routine of asking someone what they did, although we both admitted we'd used this gambit at times.

Patricia told me, 'One time I asked a dance partner what he did. He said he was a carpenter. Perhaps when I heard him I indicated a judgement—I'm not sure. I didn't intend to be negative but something came across he didn't like. So he said back to me, "Listen, lady, if it was good enough for Jesus Christ it's good enough for me."'

The story had made me laugh out loud, while also enthralling me. Patricia had shown me she was self-critical and honest, and that she could tell a good story against herself.

I was already missing her.

Sleep finally drifted over me with that memory to make me smile and relax a little.

The next day, a Saturday, began well enough. The man of the house finally appeared: Lawrie O'Callaghan, as thin and tall as his wife. He was lithe, though, with sinews that stood out just under the skin of his arms when he worked. This strength was also communicated by his stance and the way he carried himself. He was handsome in a desiccated, sun-browned bushie way.

That morning I tried to make small talk. 'It's a pleasant day. Usual this time of year?'

He ground out a reluctant response. 'Yair.'

I tried again. 'Bon said you have the key to the school. Is that so can you show me around after breakfast?'

'No. I'm busy.' After a lengthy pause, he offered the key and grunted, 'Here.'

Another try, then. 'I heard your boys talking a little earlier. Can I meet them?'

'No. They're not here.'

Clearly, Lawrie was a man of few words.

There were three boys. After Lawrie headed off that day, Jill introduced them by ushering them into the kitchen and standing them in a formal line while I sat at the table. Charlie was nearly six, Phil was seven, Michael eight. They seemed pleasant and polite, all blondies, well cared for and well-scrubbed. And I found they were, not surprisingly, children of few words.

Behind the house, Jill showed me the outdoor earth-pit dunny and the tank with its hanging bucket to draw water. The loo was a country classic, covered in vines that produced the squash as well as chokos—I didn't dare think of where the roots reached. Alongside the dunny was a chook run and some vegetable gardens, recently tilled and weed free. Jill instructed me on how to obtain hot water by filling a couple of heavy iron kettles and placing them on the front plates of the wood stove, which burned most of the time. She said, 'You can have no more than two baths a week. Or sometimes,' she added, perhaps thinking that allowance a bit lavish, 'I may tell you to have only one a week.' Weabonga has an average annual rainfall of over thirty-five inches but, as any country dweller knows, rainfall can be unpredictable. Everything in the village relied on tank water that was in short supply at times.

However, there was ample water in the tank that day, so I heated a kettle and washed and shaved before sitting down to breakfast, again eating alone: two boiled eggs, fresh from the white Leghorn or Rhode Island Reds in the yard, with some toast and a cup of tea. It was fine—but, again, I didn't realise that a precedent had been set.

After breakfast I took a walk around the village, filling in the vague picture I had formed the evening before. There were two streets: the main road, tarred for about two hundred yards, and one unpaved street off to the left. Revealed were three more houses, one with the post office located in a room at the end of its front veranda.

In the short, gravelled side street was a small weatherboard Catholic church, opened in 1926, and a ruin of what had been a hotel. Once the Royal Standard, this substantial, single-storey timber building was now falling apart and probably dangerous to enter.

On the side of the main tarred road was another tiny wooden church. A name board announced it as St George's of the Church of England. It didn't seem in as good repair as the Catholic chapel, and its surrounds showed no indication of care.

Further along to the west just before a timber bridge spanning the Swamp Oak Creek was another timber house. Then I spied a fifth, almost hidden in the bush over the other side of the creek but before the bridge. It had to be approached by a ford on the creek.

The large tin shed proved to be a village hall. It appeared to be standing upright only because the sheets of tin were leaning together closely, stabilising one another. Across the road was the gravel tennis court, fenced off by falling-down chicken wire; there were lines on the court so it appeared to be still in use.

The village, then, consisted of five poorly kept houses, all apparently with residents, two tiny chapels and a complex of huts, of which some appeared to be occupied.

Below the small section of bitumen, a clearing ran down to the creek. Studded here and there were trees the like of which I'd never before seen: huge eucalypts, broad as a Holden car and tall as a church steeple. They were gnarled and knobbed up the trunks, which rose thirty or more feet before any branches emerged.

These trees were the most impressive part of the village, which appeared to be in total decline, with any lively and successful days well past. A tenuous hold on traditions—the village hall, the tennis court, the churches—seemed to be barely maintained.

At the end of a dirt track off the main street stood the one-room school, isolated on its small rise. The grounds were in order, the hedges lining the entry path well-trimmed, the grass in the playground mown, and all seemed neat and tidy. Indeed, the school was the best-kept building in this small community, so that was a relief. The parents had surely tended its grounds in the hope that it would reopen.

4

At the Weabonga school I planned to have the children make many decisions regarding their own education. The authority and the responsibility would remain with me but, when possible, the kids would be encouraged to be self-determining. My idea—I guessed it could be seen as my educational theory, although I didn't call it that—was that opening up decisions to the children would lead to improvements both in their happiness, which I much desired for them all, and in their learning.

My training had prepared me to replicate tried-and-true classroom methods. Balmain Teachers' College was a craft institution rather than an intellectual centre, passing on the ways and means of instruction as practised for decades. Most of our lecturers had been classroom teachers and were employed at the college as much for their competency in schools as for scholarship. Their lectures were devoted either to the content of the curriculum or to methods for teaching specific material.

We all mastered basket weaving, made a jelly tray to replicate written materials—probably the only form of duplication
available in a remote school—learnt how to marble paper,
and knitted and crocheted, and we fascinated fellow public
transport passengers as we carted all such materials backwards
and forwards to college. I learnt about exclusion times for
pupils who developed scarlet fever or scabies. I could rescue
a drowning swimmer. I understood some of the rules of the
many games played by primary schoolchildren. I had failed
to learn to play well a wind instrument—the recorder—that
I later came to understand absolutely tortured many parents.
I'd also given up on the jelly tray duplication pretty quickly.
The process of preparing the gelatin in a shallow receptacle,
developing master sheets with special inks, transferring those
without blemish to the jelly's surface, and then, painstakingly,
taking off impressions on single sheets slowly and carefully,
proved to be too onerous.

The college had given me its basic lesson procedures: planned
lesson types for various methods. So I had templates for narrative
lessons, and explanation, study, reasoning, practice, drill and so
on. We trainees had tried all such lesson approaches when we
had several practice teaching sessions, assigned to a suburban
school for a few weeks during term time, under the guidance
of an experienced teacher and a visiting lecturer. In my first
appointment and with my own class, this set of model lessons
got me through most everything I thought I needed to achieve.
It was a wonderful fallback, and all my college peers agreed:
the basic lesson models supported us when we got started.

We all began our teaching career well enough but had little instruction from the college in how to be professional teachers who could independently grow and develop to our full potential, solving all the instructional and pedagogical challenges that we were sure to face in later years. Change is inevitable in schooling, but right from the outset we weren't prepared by the college to cope well with enhancements in knowledge, initiatives in procedures or improvements in content. We'd learnt almost nothing about theories of learning or curriculum development, or of competing models of education. What our lectures covered about child development was pretty minimal. And there was no introduction to academic research and how that might inform our practice and help us develop into experts.

Our training assumed that the teacher was always in charge in any classroom. The state provided many givens: a set curriculum and a well-defined timetable, specifying the exact minutes each week to be devoted to each area. It was assumed that most lessons were inductive, always led by the teacher. Discipline was strict. Self-discipline was to be encouraged, but there were firm rules and punishments for any transgression.

Schools were highly structured. There were uniforms and desks in rows. The entire school body would line up in the yard to commence the day and to re-enter the classrooms following recess and lunch. Pupils proceeded to their rooms in a military style, marching with arms swinging. They were expected to sit still and do exactly as they were told. Practice drills and rote learning predominated.

All of this was supervised by inspectors, who routinely visited each class and assessed each teacher. As our career progression depended on favourable inspectorial reports, few teachers were prepared to adopt instructional and organisational styles that challenged the accepted model.

It was into this educational milieu that I was bringing my desire for a flip-over in focus. My hope was to place the student at the centre, to be child focused, and to remove myself from the picture as much as possible so that the kids could begin to shine. After all, there was no need in our tiny school to line up in rows, and the idea that we would march anywhere was quite ludicrous. But I knew that to accomplish my own goals was going to be a challenge for me, and I wasn't sure how far I could proceed.

On our first day, following mid-morning recess, we used my blackboard illustration as a prompt to keep talking. Now we chatted about school, what the children might expect of it, and what they would enjoy. Their suggestions would be my future guide.

When Jimmy, a six-year-old, said, 'I want to be happy at school', there was a strong if subdued chorus in agreement. Many of the children said their parents had told them school days were the happiest of any life, so the kids wished for that to be true. I joined in to say, 'I agree with your mums and dads. Being together for six hours each day, five days a week, we all need to be happy in each other's company. I want you to tell me when you're happy, and if there are ever times of unhappiness we'll all work together to turn them into sunny days, with lots of smiles and laughter. Will you help me do that?'

'Golly, yes,' I heard, and, 'By jingo we will.'

Rick made a strong statement. 'We're all friends and like being with our mates. That makes school good-oh. We want to be together lots of the time.'

'I'll say,' said Will. So I asked, 'Would you like to tell me more about being with friends?'

Debbie responded thoughtfully. 'My dad says we're at school to learn and to work, so we can't be playing all the time. But there are heaps of times for playing at lunchtime and at recess. I think we'll have masses of time to be with our friends. Because Lindie and I both live out of town on a farm, we don't see much of each other except at school, so being here together all week with Vickie is just what we want.'

Tom reinforced that he was here to learn. 'When I leave school I'll be working as hard as I can to get money to buy a property of my own. I'll need to know a lot so I can earn every penny I can muster. I want school to give me a good start.'

The kids all said they not only wanted to enjoy spending time with each other but they also wanted to learn. *Good on you, mums and dads*, I thought, *for promoting the importance of education.*

I was simultaneously taking in information about the kids while noting characteristics of their speech and thought patterns. Most spoke in sentences, a good sign. A few strayed from the point, ending up somewhere unintended—but kids everywhere might do that. As a group, we'd work on clarity and precision. Two had minor speech impediments. Our youngest, Charlie, had more than a baby lisp, and I would follow up with his mum and dad, my landlord and landlady. Vickie rushed her words more than her peers and wasn't always clear in expression, but, I thought, this would improve with practice.

The children went off to lunch in relaxed spirits, no longer the anxious group who had taken some time to assemble in our schoolroom. I retrieved teaching materials from the storeroom, setting them out in stacks on my desk. Then I opened the sandwich pack that my landlady had provided: stale bread with rabbit filling. Oh no!

Every classroom in which I'd spent time—through my own education, my observation lessons at the demonstration schools attached to the teachers' college, my several weeks of practice in two suburban schools, and my two years at Kegworth—had been set up with desks in strict, straight rows, usually screwed to the floor. But these country children, with all the grades in one room, wouldn't need to be settled that way unless that was what they wanted. I decided to follow their lead on seating arrangements.

When they came back in from lunch, there was already a more inquisitive attitude among them. They were ready for what school might bring and require of them.

I asked how they'd like their room arranged. 'I'll take your suggestions, but I do need children of the same grade seated near each other, to make it easier to speak and listen. So we need Fives with Fives, Twos with Twos and so on. Everybody seated near their classmates. Okay?'

With little fuss, the children set out the desks in groups, with two tables for two facing and a two-seater stool with a back rest for each table. This arrangement would allow them to sit opposite, rather than behind each other.

Mike explained, 'We want to be able to talk together.'

'Fine,' I said, 'although you'll need to pay attention to your lessons and not chatter too much. Is that understood?'

Lots of nods was the answer. I accepted the children's seating suggestion, but left unsaid my plan to ask for changes if chatter got in the way of learning.

Four of the Grade Four boys settled in to one group of tables with a real air of ownership. Grade Three's three boys also sat happily in another group made up to a set of four when Mark, an overflow from Grade Four, joined them. Then a Grade Two boy and girl sat as a pair, making up their group of four with the two Grade One boys. The four had no difficulty in accommodating three boys with the one girl, young Susie. She just kept smiling, and she was charming me: I guessed she was charming the boys in her group as well. But that left Carol, the other girl in Grade Two, without a partner or a home base.

But not all four of the Grade Fives liked the group setting. The three girls took to it with joy but Jack, the single boy in their grade, wasn't happy. Tom also remained without a home base. He chose to sit a little removed at a desk on his own; he explained that he had to attend to his correspondence school lessons without much distraction. The young fellow again impressed me with his sensible approach, and I knew he'd be an asset to our school.

Our Grade Five boy, Jack, remained unseated, and I recognised his reluctance to sit in a group with three girls. In my Kegworth years, I'd observed that until about Grade Five, boys would rather just be with boys and not have to deal with girls or 'girly' things. Sometimes younger boys acted as though girls were disease carriers and being close to them might lead to death.

There was a spare desk, and Jack asked, 'Could I sit there by myself?'

'Sure,' I said, 'but I do need you near Vickie, Debbie and Lindie. You're our Grade Five gang, and when working with you I'll have to be able to speak quietly with all four. Is that okay?'

'All right, could we put my desk here?' Jack asked as he bumped it along to be in proximity to the two desks seating the girls.

'What do you think, girls? It suits me, Jack, if it's okay with the others.'

'Yes, yes, yes,' I heard, as the girls smiled at Jack and me.

He was happy there, smiling too. I made a mental note to monitor his involvement with his classmates; any indications of isolation would be addressed quickly.

So that left just Carol. The Grade Five girls made a suggestion. 'Could we seat Carol and Susie at a desk together? And then we could put their desk so it's between their grades, and each can work with their right class.' The older girls were keen that all the kids should be happy in their seating—I also silently noted their 'big sisterly' concern for the younger ones.

Carol and Susie grinned at each other, and everyone agreed.

All done! I'd thrown a decision open to the children, and they'd handled it simply, well and expeditiously. They had cooperated across all the age and grade divisions, and had quickly reached a solution that made them happy. In setting up their classroom, the children had been revolutionary.

Our one-room school now presented very differently to any classroom I had ever seen.

Already, the children had set themselves apart as independent thinkers but, beyond that, they had made it necessary that I address them in very different ways to the usual teacher-led, teacher-dominated 'chalk and talk'-type lessons found in all schools at the time. The children's arrangements meant I'd need to adopt a quieter, more conversational and interactive approach. What an interesting pedagogical challenge!

For the remainder of our day I invited the younger children to illustrate the stories they had told before lunch. I wanted to see how they addressed their designs, but I also planned to put up their artworks on the walls. When they arrived the next day, I wanted them to walk into a schoolroom that was clearly theirs.

As the young ones drew and painted happily, I listened to the older children read. They weren't as fluent or competent as I'd been hoping, although the inspector had alerted me to the problem of standards at Weabonga. These children were isolated in many ways, and I desired to equip them to move easily into a world beyond Weabonga if that was their chosen path. My ability to teach reading, about which I still felt a little nervous, would be vital if the kids were to progress to the point of competency by the time they moved into high school.

At home time, the children offered their goodbyes and went off between the hedges, down the path to the gate, chatting happily but quietly. They didn't hurry away, and I felt good about that.

Day one with the Weabonga children had confirmed what I'd learnt with the Kegworth kids: teaching is a profession with immediate rewards. Pupils provide constant feedback. A teacher has to set long-term goals and develop strategies to ensure all pupils reach them—some in a week, others in a month, in a term, in a year. But every day there's the satisfaction of minor accomplishments.

Feeling positive, I set to work preparing for the next day. Reliance on commercially produced materials was a given to begin with, no matter how much I wished to diminish their role, and I identified in the maths textbooks exactly what I wanted the children in each grade to attempt the next day. I then placed readers on the desks.

For our youngest boy, Charlie, who couldn't read at all, and his Grade One classmate, Jimmy, although much better prepared, everything would have to be done through direction and talking to begin, so I had early-reading and discrimination exercises ready to engage them.

Tom had shown me his secondary school correspondence lessons, formatted in weekly sets with clear targets for a student to achieve in that time. His attitude gave me confidence he was ready to guide himself through his weekly package.

Blackboard preparation was also vital, giving me a sense I was ready for anything the day might produce. Whenever I was attending to a particular class group or focusing on an individual, the board would guide the rest of the students. By my home time, a couple of hours after the children's, I had a fairly full board divided into sections: Grades One and Two, Grades Three and Four, and Grade Five. Each section had guides for reading, and for maths and English exercises, along with directions for text usage. There were suggestions for when to move between subject areas.

That afternoon set the pattern for most that followed during my first few weeks in Weabonga. After the children went home, and often early in the morning, I spent time in the schoolroom preparing for class, as I had no light source or suitable workspace at my lodgings. I tried to arrive at school just after seven and to leave no earlier than five-thirty, according to the available sunlight. With nothing to attract me to my lodgings, preparing materials and activities for the children was never a burden, and the reward was to see them eager to engage with me.

Only a few days had passed before I glimpsed advances in each child; Charlie recognised some new words, Debbie wrote a fine story, and Jack completed some maths exercises without fault. This was evidence that the school had begun well, and we appeared to be on the right track. Some of my apprehension about being teacher-in-charge had settled. Nevertheless, niggling doubts hadn't totally subsided.

Could I develop well as a teacher in this state of complete professional isolation? I'd been right to want to commence my career in a staffed school, and I was still experiencing a desire to discuss my work with other teachers.

Could I operate the one-room school well with so few supplies and so little in the way of teaching aids? I'd found significant gaps in the classroom stores, and I would have to fill them somehow.

Could I handle the social isolation? And could I develop a new life on my own, with no support from acquaintances, friends or family? The sense of being cut off from others was really sinking in; I was somewhat adrift in an unknown space.

Could I handle the stark inadequacy of my living conditions and diet? I was beginning to believe that the answer to this question was no.

My nights were troubled and I was a little unsettled by day, which darkened the clarity of my focus on the children. This wouldn't do.

5

From early on, the children and I developed routines. We paced out the days with morning intensity and afternoon languor. Mornings, when we were most alert, were filled with activities demanding close attention and persistence. Afternoons, when we'd used up much of our physical and mental resources, were devoted to more comfortable activities, such as music, gentle sports, craft and reading for pleasure.

To open each day we exchanged friendly good mornings. The children said, 'Good morning, Sir' or 'Good morning, Mr O'Brien'. I'd considered allowing them the use of my first name, but although I wanted our environment to be friendly and relaxed, I had to be seen to be in charge. My youth caused me some lingering uncertainty, and I wasn't sure if I could maintain the level of control required by the educational authorities if I permitted the kids to call me Peter. I didn't yet have a sense of personal authority that could be relied on at all times and in all matters in the school. I remained dependent on the prestige of my position: teacher-in-charge. *Carries a bit of a ring to it,* I thought. In addition, I knew that justifying any permission for the children to call me Peter would have been impossible if I'd been called on it by other teachers. It was a widely held 'truism' that formality in the teacher–pupil relationship was a necessity; any breach would have been viewed as 'letting down the side'. My self-belief was not yet strong enough to suffer that.

We pledged our loyalty once a week. 'I honour my God, I serve my Queen, I salute my Flag.' And the kids saluted the flag on one wall, next to a picture of the Queen. I was aware many commentators saw this as an expression of thought control employed by conservative governments to promote ideological goals and encourage obedience in a complacent population. I, though, was happy the children recited the pledge, even if I may have shared some minor concerns about it. The kids saw few people outside their village and its surrounds, so feeling part of a bigger event, part of the nation, was, I believed, important for them; I wanted them to have a broader image of where they might fit and what their identities might be beyond their families and Weabonga.

Almost every morning we exchanged news about ourselves. I also wanted the children to realise their lives and families were important, and that what happened in their homes and in their village and its surrounds was worthy of discussion. I hoped the kids would build respect for themselves, each other and all around them.

Much of the news was about birth: chicks, lambs, calves, pups, kittens.

Gary, from Grade Three, once told us, 'Our pet sow, Gilly, had seven piglets and most are all pink but one has brown markings.'

Sometimes news featured mercantile items.

Will, Gary's older brother, reported, 'We caught ten rabbits over the weekend. We're saving the money we get for the skins to buy a saddle.'

There were reports of dramatic happenings.

Lindie, from a sheep station out of the village along the Back Ingelba Road, surprised us with, 'A brown snake sneaked into the pantry on Saturday. Mum was terrified. We were terrified. Mum wouldn't go in there until Dad got it out.'

'How did your dad get it out?' another kid asked.

'Well, he heated up some milk and put it in a saucer on the floor just outside the pantry. Dad didn't have to wait long. The snake came slithering out. Its tongue flicked when it smelled the hot milk. Dad chopped off its head with a mattock.'

Once the news was reported, and we'd all recovered from laughter or shock, we might share a song or recite a favourite poem from the collection we quickly began to build together: something to do as one as we started the day.

After all that morning ritual, we got to work. Most pupils commenced the tasks I'd prepared for them, choosing from the blackboard instructions and using the materials set out on their desks, while I gave my attention to one group after another. In the midst of a steady morning we might take a break for chatter, for a song or to recite a poem.

Our schoolroom was designed to be inviting for the children. Their work decorated available wall spaces. Charts were in view, and any three-dimensional objects they produced were displayed on cupboards and desks. We did most of our work in that room, and it became an inclusive, vibrant place, redolent of the children and their efforts.

In good weather we ventured into the schoolyard for physical activities and, sometimes, lessons. It was spacious for our numbers and a little bare, providing plenty of room for games, sport and exercises.

We discussed having a school garden but quickly let the suggestion drop. All children reported outdoor responsibilities at home, and many assisted in—or were even in charge of—the family vegetable plot, an important source of fresh food.

Stories of snake visitors had featured since the first day, and on day three I'd drilled the children to leave the vicinity of any snake immediately, retreat to the school veranda and call the creature to my attention. I knew these kids had much better knowledge of snake behaviour than I did, but I wasn't going to put them in harm's way—this was my responsibility.

The snakes were easy to spot in the bare yard. Most were easily frightened or encouraged to continue on their slithering way, and I would watch them leave. On only one occasion was I surprised and frightened by such a visitor.

'Sir! Sir!' the children shouted. 'Snake! Snake!'

I rushed out to find a large red-bellied black snake, about eight feet in length, heading towards a hole in the earth beside the pathway to the school gate. The children would be walking there in just two hours. The snake disappeared into the cleft, but I couldn't leave it there and have the kids in peril. I went over to take a look.

Suddenly the serpent shot out of its hole, missing me by only a few inches. Snakes can turn upon themselves in a complete about-face, a good reason for never standing directly behind them.

As usual with black snakes, this one was more frightened than I. It sped off, writhing across the schoolyard to escape back into the tall grass outside the fence.

The children gave me a great cheer.

'Good on you, Sir!' Rick called.

I grinned in triumph, but I found myself shaking for some time after that encounter.

6

My breakfast on the first Sunday in the O'Callaghan house had been meditative. There was an overwhelming quietness in this home. Of course there was no television, as it couldn't have received a signal, but I hadn't heard a radio or music either. The five family members didn't chatter, and it struck me that I wasn't hearing any of the noises I expected in a home with young children.

Back in Leichhardt, most of the Kegworth kids didn't have televisions either. Television had only been introduced into Australia a few years before, in time for the Melbourne Olympic Games, and sets remained very expensive. (The large, unsightly boxes produced a grainy, black-and-white picture.) Few Kegworth families could afford them, and most judged them to be a poor investment of a family's limited funds. But those families had radios and record-players. They listened to serials and dramas, and heard several hit parades each week.

At Kegworth the kids had chatted about their favourite radio stars, singers and bands.

The Leichhardt children lived in a noisy and stimulating environment. Most of them played an organised sport on the weekend, and many went to a soccer match or a Rugby League game with their dad on a Saturday or Sunday afternoon. The children's weekly written compositions were often reruns of the Saturday afternoon movie they had seen at the local cinema.

Judging by the world of the three O'Callaghan boys, children in Weabonga had far less to see and to do than the city kids, and less to excite them and entice them to engage with learning. I wondered about the role of my school in such circumstances. Perhaps country life had compensations unavailable to town-raised children, and perhaps I might learn of these rural advantages over the two years of my appointment.

But, it seemed, not from my host family, who remained closed off towards me. I was surprised when, one Saturday morning a few weeks into my stay, with both of us a little more relaxed and in no particular hurry, Jill and I attempted to share some chatter after breakfast. Slowly I'd worked out that Jill was shy, and having a stranger living in her home was quite a challenge for her, so I'd become more careful in my approach. We were both learning about forming a better relationship.

When I innocently asked how it was that she and Lawrie had met, I received the whole story.

'Well, I grew up on the South Coast. We had aunties in Sydney so sometimes when I was twelve or older I went to spend some time with them in the school holidays. I loved my aunties but I loved being in Sydney more. It was exciting for me, as a country kid, to be in the big smoke. I'd stay for a few weeks if my aunts invited me.'

I poured out a cup of tea for each of us and nodded to encourage her to continue.

'When I was about seventeen and had been working for a while, I stayed with an auntie in Sydney for about a week. At the end of my holiday I'd said goodbye and was waiting at Central Station for the South Coast train. I had about fifteen minutes so I was just dawdling up and down, filling in time. A train pulled in beside me and all hell seemed to break loose—I could see it was a troop train, and in every carriage door and window men in uniform were leaning out. They were making a great racket, yelling, screaming and laughing, shouting and whistling. They were begging any young woman for a hug and a kiss. It seems the men were going home. Their war was over. They were demobbed and although still in uniform they were free once more.'

I urged Jill to continue; her story had me hooked.

'Young women were allowing themselves to be kissed, and everyone on the platform was laughing and cheering. One young bloke pulled me into a carriage and gave me a hug and then a kiss. Golly, he was handsome. I thought I'd be catching my train in a few minutes so I grew a bit cheeky and kissed him right back.'

That was it! Fate had intervened in her life.

'Lawrie and I met in an extraordinary way. I thought it meant to be, so I gave him my address and he gave me his.'

Lawrie and Jill had corresponded by letter from their homes and quickly made arrangements to marry at the Sydney Registry

Office, a sort of halfway point. Some of her Sydney relatives attended, but no one from Lawrie's Weabonga family was able to make the trip.

Jill said, 'I knew little of Lawrie and nothing of his home or his family. I just knew I had to be with him no matter what. We came to Weabonga immediately following the marriage. I've not left it since.'

I was concerned to hear that she'd never been back to her South Coast home or family in fifteen years, but kept my worries to myself.

Upon learning that Lawrie was a war veteran, I wondered whether his experiences in the war had been an ongoing burden to him. I remembered a paternal uncle who had been so damaged emotionally and psychologically in his late teens by his First World War experiences that he'd never recovered; he had lived out his life in reduced, isolated and sometimes distressing circumstances. Lawrie clearly wasn't as compromised as my uncle had been, but had his memories of the Second World War similarly contributed to his silences?

Jill's tale provoked my own musings that Saturday evening. After I climbed into bed on the front veranda, I couldn't stop thinking about my immediate future. Was I just falling into a life I hadn't sought and wasn't really welcoming? I'd grown more confident that I could handle the needs of the little school, but I was getting more stressed about my accommodation arrangements. And I had some other concerns to do with Patricia.

My drowsy mind had me wondering if she was thinking of our friendship in the same way that I did. Was I as special to her as she was to me?

Towards the end of the previous year, when we'd known each other for about seven months, Patricia had decided to move interstate. I was quite unhappy about this but couldn't speak up against it, particularly as I'd just received my transfer to Guy Fawkes.

Patricia had, by then, beaten me to independence, moving away from her grandparents to live in a shared flat in North Bondi. I had arrived there one night unannounced; I'd just desired to catch up with her, and, by then, spontaneous visits weren't unusual for us.

That night I found another young fellow sitting on the sofa. He was quite unknown to me. *My spot*, I thought, and I was shocked when it became clear he was visiting my friend, not either of her flatmates.

Quickly I saw him for what he was: a competitor! He and I spoke little, and only through Patricia. The atmosphere grew strained, but I was determined to show grace and composure; I didn't want my friend to make any negative judgements of me. I couldn't care what the 'bounder' and 'cad' thought. The evening wore on. He, the dastardly one, sat on. I sat on. Matters dragged and the conversation was painful and slow. He wouldn't leave. I wouldn't leave. Midnight went by. Then one o'clock. As it was approaching two, he gave up and said his farewells. What relief—my persistence had won the day.

Would I, though, win in the longer term?

The next time I met up with Patricia, she reassured me about the young fellow. 'Look, he's a decent guy and very respectful, but he's bothering me too much for a date. The truth is, I have no interest in him in that way, and his requests have become quite annoying. I'd like to get away from him.' She added, 'I've been thinking I'll move to Melbourne for a while. You know, all my friends in the Young Elizabethan drama group are going there—they want to try becoming professionals.'

I was knocked down by Patricia's sudden application of a feather. But, trying to accept her choice as calmly as I could, I helped her with the move.

By the time I arrived in Weabonga, we were regularly in touch. Each of us expressed interest in how the other was finding their new location, and we reported our tentative steps into our new lives. Facing similar challenges was bringing us closer together, I hoped, as I tried to view our separation optimistically.

But maybe, I conjectured as I lay awake on the veranda, I was seeing our friendship through rose-coloured glasses. Maybe I was deluding myself.

7

In my understanding, children's development of reading skills was dependent on modelling from proficient readers, lots of free and supervised practice, and a gradual increase in the number and variety of words they could recognise easily by sight. Children needed to comprehend what they were reading and have a strategy for tackling new words. So, I thought, maybe the Weabonga kids hadn't experienced sufficient of any of those necessities, and I'd have to make up for these gaps.

At college I'd been trained in the whole-words and phonics methods for reading instruction, and I had relied on them in my first classes at Kegworth. As I understood it, all schools and all teachers were sure to be employing a mix of these approaches. The whole-words method depends on the smooth build-up of word recognition: an increasing store of words the child recognises at once and reads fluently. Phonics requires the child to deconstruct a word into letter or syllabic components, sound out letters or letter groups (phonemes), then reconstruct the word by combining these separate sounds. Even to describe the process makes the phonics approach seem difficult.

At Kegworth a few children had taken naturally and easily to reading—lucky kids. They required no teaching, the strategy being to keep them interested in what they read, as they developed by themselves easily enough. I found that Susie certainly and Jimmy possibly might fit that profile. *Hooray for them*, I thought. The other Weabonga children, though, weren't as fortunate. They had to construct and remember a word-recognition library, and they needed practice, practice, practice and lots of revision. I believed they could become quite proficient readers if they worked at it and received appropriate support. What made the situation a little more challenging was that these Weabonga kids seemed hesitant about reading, and they didn't appear to have mastered large numbers of words by sight. *I'll have to assist these tardy kids as much as possible*, I thought. *They're going to need most of my time.*

I'd also found that a small group experienced difficulty in realising that words existed or in recognising the printed shapes or letter patterns of words. Associating a name with that pattern or word shape was a difficult chore for such children. Early on I assessed that Charlie, Gary and Vickie would need extra support. *Here's where phonics might help*, I thought hopefully—I wasn't sure. My confidence in my ability to teach reading was still low, even after two years at Kegworth.

But what of my desire for a child-centred approach? What about having the children make as many decisions as possible when it came to their reading? That might lead the way, I realised, to a kind of reading instruction that suited me.

Underlying everything child centred was the goal of enjoying ourselves—reading wasn't to be a test but rather a treat. We all learn to read because this skill opens routes to knowledge and pleasure. So, I decided, learning to read should be both comfortable and happy in our small school.

Our two littlies, Charlie and Jimmy, were my initial focus, and we commenced with their first primer. In it, the boys found simple stories.

> See it go.
>
> See it go up.
>
> Up, up, up.
>
> Jump up, Baby.
>
> Jump up.
>
> Up, up, up.
>
> Jump up.

Well, I found that less than thrilling, and so did both boys! Deciding to try something different—to be child centred—we set out to create their own story on which to practise. We were dealing with the adverb or preposition 'up', so I asked the boys what went up.

Charlie said, 'A magpie.'

Jimmy said, 'A crow.'

I asked, 'To where did those birds go up?'

Both called out, 'In the air, into the sky.'

'How did they go up?'

'They flew up into the sky,' both again cried.

'Why were they up in the sky?'

'To look about and find good things to eat,' came a whip-quick suggestion from Jimmy.

In his slow, almost wistful way, Charlie added, 'Birdth fly 'cause thas whath birdth do. They were doing things birdth do.'

With little encouragement Jimmy and Charlie worked out an 'up' story, and I wrote it down for them.

Up in the Sky
Up, up.
Jimmy says crow and Charlie says magpie.
Up in the sky, they fly real high.
What did they spy from up in the sky?
They spied you and they spied me.
We were all on the ground you see.
Up, up. Up they go.

No Nobel Prize for Literature here, but the boys loved it, read it avidly, learnt to recognise the words quickly and each built their sight-word library with success.

Their short story had new words for them that we wrote on flashcards:

magpie crow real sky high spy spied ground see

As can happen in a small one-room school, through all students being in close proximity, everyone had observed the littlies become authors. All were delighted for them, adopting the story as a prized school composition. The tiny chaps' creativity motivated all. Two of our Grade Twos, Steve and Susie, created another story section—but rather than up, they wanted to go down.

Down in the Ground
Down, down.
Steve says miner, down in the ground.
Digging so lots of gold might be found.
Susie says worm, down in the soil,
All day and all night she will toil and toil.
Down, down, down in the ground.

This was also well received and, spontaneously, Lindie began to sing to her own tune: 'Jimmy says crow and Charlie says magpie. Up in the sky, they fly real high . . .' Sandra, Vickie and Debbie quickly began to sign along. The girls gave their song a sort of calypso beat, catchy and easily picked up. Within minutes everyone, including me, had joined in. Charlie and Jimmy hopped up and, flapping their arms, flew around. Some kids warbled, others cawed; bird sounds filled the room.

These 'up' and 'down' stories were the beginning of a useful and happy routine. From their success onwards, we often composed and read our own stories.

Similarly to all schoolchildren in all NSW schools at the time, the Weabonga kids—apart from Tom—had flashcards, and sets of them began to accumulate.

For the Twos we added a new set the day of the 'down' story.
ground   found   digging   gold   soil   toil
The Twos also had cards with words from another favourite story that they, and even the Threes, returned to often.
rolling   plum   can't   catch   off   look   world

For Grade Four we stored away many, many words, gathered from the stories and poems they enjoyed.

piper   stept   slept   smiling   quiet   Hamelin   magic

For that story Rick asked, 'Are "stepped" and "stept" the same? Why does the story spell "stept" that way?'

How else would a teacher respond? 'Well spotted, Rick, and such a great question.'

The Fives loved alerting each other to new and, perhaps, difficult words. These four had understood early that their initiative was welcome and appreciated, and they would often print out new flashcards for one another and then arrange to drill and test themselves. Time spent on reading activities flashed by for all of them. They were becoming quietly confident readers—even Vickie was progressing. When I could, I spent time with each of them, boosting their skills. Those bonny kids enjoyed any books with an Australian theme, setting or characters: those by Colin Thiele, Joan Phipson, Kylie Tennant and Patricia Wrightson were all much loved.

rough   gnarled   station   responsibility   coot   reckon   stranger Meccano   rabbiting

How thankful I was for the strength of those four kids. Their success released me to spend more time with the others, including the five boys in Grade Four: Mike, Will, Rick, Mark and Joe. They were all making steady progress, but I still wanted to give them as much attention and assistance as possible. They also read aloud to Tom when he had time to devote to the younger ones, which he relished doing.

Most of the content of our reading program would have been recognised by any teacher and most students at the time.

We did loads of practice: flashcard drills, matching and sorting shapes, drawing letters and words, practising spelling, you read/I read. But because we set out to enjoy reading, we not only created our own unique stories but also chose to read material that challenged and entertained us.

At Weabonga we also focused on success. With our child-centred approach, this was a necessity for us. Children making mistakes wasn't part of my strategy—I hoped they would love reading and soon become competent, building confidence as proficient learners. In my view, a strategy of having children learn from their errors seldom led to progress and, as a teaching method, never appealed. I had observed that kids typically didn't know they'd made an error or why it had occurred; even fewer had enough insight to self-correct.

'I've never seen any important academic learning follow from errors,' I told myself.

'Isn't that a bit of a stretch?' I prompted my conscience.

'No, not really,' I answered. 'I'll back myself on that, and we can't go far astray anyway—nothing problematic about making certain the kids can correctly complete their reading exercises, is there?'

I didn't view this internal conversation as idiosyncratic. Having no other adult to talk with, I sometimes chatted away to myself when the children had gone home. It would have been terribly lonely otherwise.

My observation was that school learning wasn't self-correcting. I knew with certainty most children learnt to avoid a hot flame once burnt. But, I asked myself, 'How do children learn to self-correct when they believe 24 x 5 equals 130, or it's fine to write, "John and me went to town"?'

I'd seen at Kegworth that frequent errors could prove destructive to a child's self-image as a capable learner, harming their willingness to engage in new learning tasks. I wanted no such challenge for our Weabonga pupils. And because I was attending to five different grades at once, I didn't have time to retrace lessons and go over material.

Of course, even the best-prepared learners will make errors. The kids needed to be prepared to overcome mistakes rather than to be put off by them, as all children need to become persistent in the face of challenges: that's one of life's most important lessons, and I wanted to assist them in learning it. But they were country kids and one of the important differences between them and city kids would assist them.

They had witnessed lots of setbacks and had observed their families learning to cope with abrupt changes. They'd seen losses of ewes and lambs in birthing, and the loss of vegetables and fruit from pest infestations in their hard-worked gardens; they'd witnessed foxes feasting on their chook flocks, and all had endured a lack of water due to drought. Some of these kids had seen their pet lamb served up as a grilled chop—no failure in our school was going to present them with a larger challenge than that.

So the Weabonga children learnt that from time to time they could be stumped by new reading material—but that through sounding out words and developing a clearer understanding of the story, they could find ways around blockages. Additionally,

I made sure not to introduce reading challenges that a child couldn't overcome.

The accumulating flashcards were kept in shoeboxes, beginning with sets for each grade and then, eventually, for each child. The kids practised word recognition from the flashing of the cards, with me, on their own or with a classmate. Vickie, say, would compete in a friendly match-up with Debbie, Lindie or Jack.

And all the time we were asking how, what, when, why, where and who—Rudyard Kipling's 'six honest serving-men' of learning—about all our stories. Gradually stocks of comprehension exercises associated with stories in magazines and texts, but also self-compositions, began to accumulate in their own shoeboxes.

Children in the more senior grades came to be independent and proficient in working their way through the cards, recording their answers for me to talk over with them. I could depend on the Fours and Fives to complete such exercises with little fuss and a happy buzz, allowing me more time with littlies who couldn't be so self-directing.

A college lecturer had told us that by primary school graduation, a student needed a stock of two to three thousand words they could immediately recognise by sight. That gave me and the kids a sensible goal.

By the time Mary and Merrilyn joined us as Kindergarten enrollees in the second year, my confidence in reading instruction had grown. Through observing the success of the child-centred approach, and having built up a good stock of reading aids and materials with the older children, I was ready to assist the two little ones. Both were friendly, happy girls, eager to fit in and like school. The older children cared for and, sometimes, spoiled them.

⌒

My first weeks at the school were productive and enjoyable, and I felt we'd made a good start. Away from the schoolroom, though, my life was increasingly problematic. My unease and unhappiness were debilitating—and, without doubt, my living conditions were to blame. I no longer felt able to influence the important choices in my life.

My friendship with Patricia was becoming a source of calmness and strength: my niggling doubts about her affection had diminished. We'd been keeping in touch through frequent letters and were soon speaking on the phone every Saturday morning.

No home in the village had a telephone, but a public phone was easily accessed on the post office veranda. From that PO exchange also ran two party lines: one south-east, following the Niangala Road, and the other north-west, following the Limbri Road. Sometimes the party line was opened at the exchange and a ring tone was sent to indicate that anyone could pick up and take part in the call: a sort of broadcast. That had taken place on the Saturday after my arrival, and so all the district knew of my appointment to the school and my name.

Phone calls were expensive then, and all calls from Weabonga were by long distance, which carried even higher costs. The expense weighed on my mind, and I had to make hard choices, making as few calls as possible. This soon began to affect my relationships with people back in the city. I wrote many letters but knew these weren't as powerful as hearing a person's voice. The cost of communication made me even more isolated.

All the grazing properties had phones, sharing a party line with eight or more users. It was possible for anyone to listen in on any call on that line, so each user had a signal, such as four rings for the Browns or three rings for the Smiths— supposedly, only the intended recipient would pick up. I was told, though, that everyone suspected everyone else of occasionally eavesdropping.

On the way to Weabonga, Bon had suggested I shouldn't divulge on a party line anything I wanted to keep to myself. 'Never talk with your sheila on a party-line phone, Pete, if you want to keep it private,' had been his unsought advice.

Patricia was always interested to hear about the children in my care, and I loved that she had such regard for them. One Saturday from the public phone on the PO veranda, a private line, I told her how our past week had been one of intense work on reading—and how inadequate I felt about helping the kids gain proficiency. She responded by telling me of her own start in reading.

Patricia had lived with her beloved grandparents from a young age, and her grandfather would read aloud to her every day. One of their favourites was *Ginger Meggs*, a comic strip in a daily newspaper. Patricia told me, 'One day, when I was three going on four, I was sitting beside Grandfather on the couch and he was reading *Ginger Meggs*. As he read, he'd run his finger along the line, pointing to each word as it was pronounced.

It was my habit to try to follow on the page where he was in the story. So I knew words had meaning.

'On this day Grandfather was just saying, "Ginger said," when I suddenly knew that word right there on the page was the one he'd said. Before Grandfather could do so, I just read aloud the words on the rest of the line. He was astounded! He began getting me books, introducing me to stories like *Anne of Green Gables*. We sat reading together on the couch quite often. He'd run his finger along each line to help me know where we were.'

By the time Patricia commenced school, at age five, she was reading with some facility. But a nun at her country convent school refused to believe it. The woman scolded, 'You are a very naughty girl—you have just memorised those words and you are not reading them. That is cheating.' It wasn't until Grandfather visited the school that the nun was convinced a child just commencing Kindergarten could be a reasonably proficient reader.

This story delighted me and reaffirmed the vital importance of nurture in the care of children. I was also charmed by what it revealed about Patricia's abilities. I still had trouble believing that this bright, competent and empathetic girl was attracted to me. How lucky was I?

8

On my third Sunday morning with the O'Callaghans, I noticed Lawrie preparing to cut the high grass in the field next to the house. At the back door, he began by sharpening two large scythes on a grindstone. These implements each had a six-foot-long curved, wooden handle, two smaller handholds, and a three-foot metal blade. Except in a Jean-François Millet painting of nineteenth-century French peasants—Millet prints had hung in my sixth-grade convent school classroom—I'd seen nothing like them before and was intrigued. I offered Lawrie my help, also hoping I might finally be able to strike up a friendly conversation.

Lawrie showed me how to cut in a long sweeping motion and, a rhythm established, slowly advance by reaping along an imagined row. The work was tiring and I soon needed gloves, but we kept going. The grass would be ready to be gathered into stooks after being left to dry for a day or two.

As I scythed, I occasionally looked up to take in the surrounding hills with their thick woods. I felt at one with Millet's
labourers, although not at one with those of Vincent van Gogh,
as his paintings of reapers featured colours more varied and
vibrant than those around me. I didn't see the golds, reds, pinks
and mauves of Van Gogh's palette; the bush at Weabonga had
darker tones of charcoal, silver, olive and navy-blue, among the
dense, almost black greens. That I saw beauty in the shadowy
woods against the bright blue sky struck me forcibly.

Lawrie could have kept scything all day, but he sat with me
for a smoko and broke his customary silence. He pointed just
down the hill and said, 'Tennis this afternoon.'

'Who plays?' I asked. 'Can I join in?'

'Yair.'

Until then I'd been spending Sunday afternoons at the school
getting ready for the week ahead. Unable to see the community
tennis court from inside the schoolroom, I hadn't noticed it
was in use, so Lawrie's terse advice was a bit of a revelation.

I felt I had established a slightly better relationship with
Lawrie although little had been said. Mostly it had just been
the two of us reaping in tandem, in silence.

There were about eight adults in the tennis party. All knew
who I was, so they greeted me with a warm welcome as they
introduced themselves. I'd met a few when they brought
their kids on enrolment morning, but several introduced
themselves for the first time. They all wanted to tell me how
absolutely delighted they were that I had come to town and

how important it was, for all at Weabonga, that the school had reopened.

'Our small school is the glue that holds this place together,' Vic Teegan said. He had a sheep property about ten miles out on the back road to Ingelba, the nearest community to Weabonga.

'Indeed,' added Tony Wallace, whose property was also around ten miles out of the village but on the Limbri Road, in the opposite direction to Vic's place. 'Anything that happens in this community usually comes about through the school. We were all terribly worried when there was no teacher for us at the beginning of the year. We'd heard threats that our kids might be made to bus down to Dungowan. Well, we couldn't accept that—no good for the kids and no good for us. We'd lose the community if the school closed.'

The tennis was arranged as games of doubles, with each game being only one set, ensuring frequent changes of players. The pairs were drawn from a hat. Everyone played a couple of games, then all shared an afternoon tea with homemade cakes and biscuits. It was warm and pleasant, an excellent introduction to the wider community.

Although the players weren't overly chatty, they managed to extract lots of information from me. Straightforwardly, not in the least bit embarrassed by the personal nature of the information they sought, they put queries to me, and expected answers.

'Tell us something about yourself, Peter,' said a village mum, June Baulderstone.

'How long have you been teaching?' asked Monica Whitworth, another village mother.

June and Monica were sisters-in-law, each with two boys at the school.

I was happy to be interrogated and offered everything they wanted to know. These parents had placed their children in my care—they had a right to know all about me.

In turn, I asked lots of questions about Weabonga. I confirmed there were just five homes in the village, and that the group of huts up the hill was inhabited: an elderly brother and sister had lived there all their lives. I decided to go up and introduce myself to the pair in the near future.

All the village homes had primary-aged children, and the parents seemed to be in their mid-thirties to late forties. Outside the village there were some older children of school age, but these kids were either at boarding school or were residents in the Tamworth hostels for secondary children during term time.

All the men of the village were day labourers, taking whatever work was offered on properties in the surrounding area. They didn't travel too far from home, finding enough employment on nearby stations to provide for their families. All could shear but chose not to spend weeks away in shearing teams. The men could turn their hands to most tasks needed on a grazing property. The village families also kept a few head of stock—'killers', they called them—on the town common situated over the bridge and around the next couple of bends off the Limbri Road; these animals provided meat for the family meals.

The village women, all wives and mothers, were fully employed in their home duties.

'We do what we can with what we've got,' explained June, 'but there's lots to do and we're always chasing our tails.'

From working with the kids I'd already come to understand that their families lived precarious lives, sustaining themselves through intermittent work and whatever food they could produce. These weren't layabout or hillbilly people but hardworking folk, doing their best to provide for their kids and build a better future for them. Most were probably in Weabonga because housing was cheap, and home ownership offered some stability in challenging circumstances.

I had learnt some Weabonga history from Bon during the drive in his mail car, but I heard much more that first tennis afternoon. There had been mining of quartz reef gold in the area for quite a period, and I was advised to be careful walking through the bush as there were still many shafts and most had no protective fencing. Stock was sometimes lost into such shafts. Bill Whitworth advised, 'Watch where you go, mate. Keep your eyes open as you walk. Always look around and know where your next step'll go. You fall down one of those shafts and we'll never clap eyes on you again.'

For a while the gold had attracted a large population—five hundred or more people had lived in the village at times. There had been a number of active hotels and several shops as well as a police station and a courthouse for petty sessions. The former police station was now the relatively substantial home across from the tennis court.

Max Baulderstone pointed to a large old chimney standing isolated on the hill above St George's church and told me, 'That was a hotel and billiard room. When the gold was flowing, the village was a busy little place.'

I was surprised to hear that one of the corrugated-iron huts, the home of the elderly siblings whom I'd yet to meet, had been a courthouse. The story was that the father of this pair had been the resident magistrate, and when he'd died unexpectedly his children had somehow become stranded and were living out their lives in relative poverty.

The four players from grazing properties described a little of their way of life. Weabonga was in a high-rainfall area, and the weather patterns were fairly consistent. Grass was normally lush and nutritious, so the locals pastured high stock numbers. Each property in the area was about fifteen hundred to two thousand acres in extent and carried around three to four thousand sheep, around two head per acre, with some cattle. The wool was quite fine, not top quality but always attractive to foreign buyers, so when wool prices were high the properties returned significant incomes. The homesteads were quite substantial, machinery was in good order, and an older Teegan child had been sent off to private boarding high school.

Max reported, 'Some of our village kids have done real well at our little school and have been chosen to go on to Farrer for high school.'

Farrer was a selective state high school at Nemingha, about twenty miles away near Tamworth, where the children had been boarders. Max seemed proud of having some pupils qualify for a selective school, and the nods of Bill and Vic confirmed what I was suspecting: the Weabonga families wanted their children to do well and to progress in our village school.

Their comments were designed to let me know they would be watching me. That didn't put me off; I was pleased they shared my high expectations for the kids.

It was clear from everyone's interactions around the tennis that they enjoyed friendly, respectful relationships, whether they were landowners or day labourers. I'd enjoyed getting to know them a little, our interactions wonderfully welcome after three weeks of almost no communication with adults.

A little later I found that meeting June Baulderstone and Monica Whitworth had been a gift, as they joined the Parents and Citizens Group that we set up to support the school. Vic Teegan and Marie Wallace also came to the P and C whenever they could.

I'd very much appreciated the tennis club's afternoon tea. That evening Jill served up the usual—baked rabbit with squash. Lord save me!

9

After assessing the children's reading levels, I evaluated their knowledge and skills in mathematics. Again, I wasn't surprised to find they were all somewhat behind the level expected of them by the NSW curriculum. Unlike their lack of competent reading skills, though, their being behind in maths didn't perturb me much. I'd found that, given the right opportunities, time, appropriate tasks and encouragement, primary-aged children could quickly catch up and even get well ahead of anything expected of them in this area.

My goals with maths learning mirrored those with reading: success, enjoyment, child focus and child inclusion. Those goals had to sit within the state curriculum, so I didn't expect we'd be doing much that was dramatically different to what might be seen in any primary classroom.

The curriculum was quite specific and rigid. When the inspector came to call, he would test what the children had covered against each prescribed area, then estimate what they'd achieved under my tuition. I found all the curricula useful, giving me direction and goals, and I planned to be always ready for an inspectorial visit—I didn't want the kids or me to be found wanting in any way.

Being without colleagues, I keenly felt the need for external, independent benchmarks to assess our progress. What I really wanted was a valid and reliable comparison to other institutions, perhaps through a state or national assessment; this could have provided vital information about my students. How good it would have been to know how we were travelling at Weabonga compared to schools elsewhere.

The maths texts I'd found in the school store would be the basis of most of our activities, supplemented with activities of my own design. In the evenings I developed task cards with graduated exercises and problems for all the major maths concepts and processes the kids needed to master. These cards were intended to build, inexorably, success on success.

As with the reading cards, we kept the maths sets easily accessible in shoeboxes. With my help the children kept track of their progress on a personal chart as they moved from early to later cards. At a glance each knew what had been covered, what they had achieved and where they might go next; with a second glance, an assessment of their attainment of curricula requirements could be made. These charts weren't meant to encourage competition but to be a picture of individual progress. If there was any competition, it was only from the children challenging themselves.

What we developed was a program for each pupil that depended on having materials organised and close at hand. The content had a local flavour as most of these materials involved activities based on the children's interests, needs and questions. We held small group instruction for those areas where I hadn't yet been able to create such individual materials.

All these country kids were fascinated by numbers. The boys in particular asked about them often and were keen to find answers. Jack and Rick would enquire about the numbers of sheep per acre, sheep shorn in a day, and fleece weights. Will and Joe wanted to know what a shearer would earn at one shilling and sixpence per sheep if they shore eighty-five sheep in a day. Mike and Gary asked questions of grain yields per acre, and Mark questioned the number of rabbit skins needed to make a pound weight. Phil urgently asked one Monday morning what might be earned by selling five pounds of rabbit skins to the hide merchant—the rabbit-trapping operation he and Mike ran had a bumper weekend, I presumed.

The girls asked questions of a different nature. Sandra spoke of the method for working out the skeins of knitting wool needed for a pattern. Lindie queried the lengths of material needed for a hand-sewn skirt. Debbie asked about the quantity of butter for a marble cake. Vickie queried the time it would take to roast a chicken weighing two pounds two ounces. I treated these questions in the same way as those of the boys; they simply revealed this society's sharply delineated expectations for each gender.

Some of our maths task cards mentioned a nearby sheep property: 'What's the area in acres of Finn's paddock measuring five hundred by five hundred yards?'

Others were set on a village family and home: 'How many skeins of wool would the knitter need for a pair of socks if each sock took two and one-half skeins?'

'Here's a recipe for Mrs Wallace's pound cake. When you add the weight of all the ingredients, does it really weigh a pound?'

'How long would one hundredweight of laying mash last for the O'Callaghans' chooks if Phil fed them two pounds' weight of mash a day?'

Admittedly, as Tom's lessons came to him prepared, I only had to create an individualised maths program for seventeen pupils compared to thirty, the usual class size at the time, but even at Kegworth I'd been able to individualise much of the maths instruction in my classes of thirty-five students or more. The challenge here at Weabonga was that I had to account for five grades. I was also worried that simply due to their geographical isolation these children were at a disadvantage to city kids, and I didn't want to add to such disadvantage by not having my pupils achieve as highly as they could. So we voyaged on together, tackling the curriculum in a steady routine, allowing the kids' interests to direct us whenever possible.

One day we were all fascinated to notice and observe a crop-duster plane distributing superphosphate to an acreage we could see over the creek and up the hill from the school. This was the first time a local grazier had decided to aerial spread his paddocks, and the whole district was focused on the possibilities for pasture improvement.

While we all watched from the veranda Jack asked, 'What's the load each trip?'

'What's it cost per load?' queried Tom.

Will wanted to know, 'How many trips did we see?'

'So how much super is being spread?' quizzed Mike.

'Okay,' said Jack, 'how much super was spread on each acre in that paddock?'

'Which airstrip is the plane flying from?' murmured Vickie.

'What distance is that to the paddock we can see?' wondered Debbie.

Then Joe asked, 'If there were ten trips, how many miles did it fly?'

Number questions were posed almost ad infinitum—and the kids craved answers. Maths lessons for several days had crop dusting as their starting point, and the children's interest didn't wane.

Magic moments like these paid the greatest dividends for me. I found it sublime to observe the children's minds totally engaged, all synapses firing, concentration at a peak, really working hard because they wanted to know, to understand, to learn, to grow. That isn't to diminish the genuine efforts the kids were ready to expend most of the time. If I asked them to engage, they did. But whenever I saw the excitement of learning in their eyes or the thrill of an 'aha!' moment on their faces, I wanted this feeling to go on forever. Of course, if it had it would have quickly worn us all out. But, oh, it was good when it happened.

10

After five weeks with Lawrie and Jill, I stopped eating their rabbit and squash. I asked Bon to purchase a large box of shortbread biscuits, and began to live off those along with a couple of boiled eggs and a slice of toast each morning provided by Jill. Bon hadn't been surprised by my order and hinted he understood the reason; he probably did, as he claimed to have a number of relatives in Weabonga. Vic or Jan Teegan brought me fresh milk each morning from their farm when they dropped off Lindie and Susie. The Teegans also didn't seem surprised by my request and hinted that they understood the reason. *So,* I thought, *the whole district must know of my plight.*

I hadn't told the tennis families of my woes—I didn't want to appear to be complaining about a village family, particularly when their children were in my care. However, I had been informed, subtly and by inference, that my landlords were the only family that would provide accommodation for me. The other village families had crowded houses, and the graziers wouldn't have been able to spare the time to deliver and retrieve me each day. To ensure the school would be reopened, Lawrie and Jill had stepped forward to do their best; I understood that.

It was widely believed that my rent would give them significant financial assistance, and I understood that as well. On the first morning I'd asked Jill how she would like to receive my board, and she had said, 'Once a month, as a cheque. Just leave it open. Don't make it out to anyone. That'll work best for us. We can cash it in any shop then—any shop in town will do that. So that's easiest.' From that response I understood that my rent money would remain without a trail as far as Lawrie and Jill were concerned, and that was fine by me. They needed every penny they could get for their boys.

Over the first month the family hadn't gone to town, but when I delivered my first payment they set off for a day in Tamworth. On their return I noticed they carried in a number of bags and packages. Unfortunately, it seemed none contained food items.

On a diet of two eggs, six biscuits and a couple of glasses of milk a day, I began to deteriorate. Within a short time, sharp and persistent stomach pains began. This became a constant nagging that reminded me insistently of my discontent.

By the time Easter approached, on the third Sunday in April, I was feeling quite desperate: I had no company of my own age, I had an improper diet, I spoke with other adults only on Sunday afternoons for a few hours at most, and I lived in a tar-paper cubby. I loved being with the children, but that wasn't enough to make up for everything else.

I remembered fondly my college classmates and Kegworth colleagues, as well as the group of friends I'd grown up with. Even my six obligatory months in the military—in National Service barracks packed with hundreds of young guys—began to look more attractive in hindsight.

Until now I'd always been surrounded by friends of my own age. I had a lively, at times exciting and always fulfilling social life. My church youth group met one night each month, and enjoyed outings and activities together between times. In winter I played in their Rugby League team, which gave me an opportunity to meet lots of young people from other suburban church groups.

I had a closer group of five male friends, my mates, some of whom I'd known since Kindergarten, and we spent lots of time together. All of us played in the local footy team, and three of us were keen dancers and went out a few nights a week to suburban dance halls. We enjoyed the music and the dancing, and these nights also gave us a chance to meet young women. On the non–dance nights, if we weren't taking young ladies on a date, my mates met to play billiards and share a few drinks in a city pool hall, or to play tennis on a floodlit court.

My problems at home in Sydney had been to do with finding privacy, not enduring loneliness. I had four siblings, and my gregarious mother frequently hosted guests; sometimes friends from the country stayed for days or weeks at a time. We had a largish extended family, and cousins and aunts came to see us often. My mother had been born and grew up in Ireland, so there was much music, singing and dancing, with jigs, reels, the Blackbird and the Irish hornpipe. Every few months my parents arranged a music night: a *ceilidh*. About twenty of their friends would come, three of whom brought their fiddles. They'd move the dining-room table and rugs out of the way before beginning their Irish set dances, with space for two sets of eight dancers each in the cleared room. As soon as we children had sufficient rhythm and knew the steps, we were encouraged to join in. We loved it all: the harmonies, the happiness, the vivacity and sheer good humour. Between dances there was lively conversation and all were included, so we children learnt to take part, in a respectful way, with people of all ages. On some other evenings my father would sit for an hour or so playing the piano contentedly, either Thomas Moore's melodies or similar Irish songs. Dad had a pleasant tenor voice and would often sing along, accompanying himself. So there was always music, laughter and chatter in our home.

After a couple of months in Weabonga, I was quite bereft and needed a circuit-breaker. I decided to return to Sydney to spend the Easter holiday at home, eating three proper meals a day while catching up with family and friends—including Patricia, who was coming up to Sydney from Melbourne. I'd get a lift out with Bon in the mail car, then catch the train.

Ringing Mr Flood, I explained my intentions and the reasons the school would not reopen until eleven on the Wednesday morning. I spelt out why I needed the break. When he heard of my living conditions, he became very sympathetic and expressed his regret for having placed me in this situation. But he didn't offer any help.

The long weekend at home was the reward I'd thought it would be, allowing me to catch up with everyone and engage in happy, light-hearted events. There were lots of lively conversations but I spoke little to my family of my living arrangements; there was nothing my loved ones could do to alleviate them, and they would only worry.

I spent some wonderful time with Patricia and chose to share only some of my woes with her too. She'd travelled up to visit her family but also to see me, and I appreciated her readiness to arrange time for us to get together. All indications were that she returned my feelings, which did much to calm my worries and feed my hopes.

On the Saturday the two of us had dinner at Ling Nam's, a basement restaurant on King Street. We enjoyed the calm atmosphere, our table for two conducive to an intimate tête-à-tête. A small, relaxed orchestra played danceable numbers, and we moved on and off the dance floor as our courses were served and dishes taken away. We ordered sparkling red wine, its fizz elevating our happiness.

I told my five mates more of the Weabonga reality, and they told me to ditch the whole arrangement and demand that the Department of Education redress these appalling circumstances. In their opinion, no Australian in 1960 needed to accept what I was being asked to tolerate. *That's what mates are for,* I thought.

As I travelled back from Limbri in the mail car beside the Swamp Oak Creek—asking often for the car to stop so I could hop out to escape the noxious fumes of a farting kelpie who lay at the driver's feet—I decided my situation must improve. I knew now I had to resolve the situation myself. If my accommodation remained as it was, I would ask the inspector for a transfer. I'd give it until the May school vacation, coming up in less than a month. The challenges of Weabonga had forced me to grow as a person, and I was now prepared to speak up on my own behalf.

The inspector had told me that he'd found it hard to keep the school staffed. Now I understood why.

11

I'd brought back a couple of books from my own childhood-library, and in the days after Easter I introduced the younger children to Dorothy Wall's *Blinky Bill* series and the older group to Ethel Pedley's *Dot and the Kangaroo*. I'd chosen these books because of the children's eager response to any story featuring animals; I also judged them to be a little above the reading capabilities of the kids for whom they were intended, so I read them aloud.

The littlies just loved Blinky and his exploits; they made several requests for me to get on with the next instalment. But Dot didn't receive the same joyful reception, so the older children and I formed a plan for me to cease reading if they said they weren't enjoying it enough to continue. *Fair enough*, I thought, and this had given me a chance to talk with them about what we loved from our reading and what we might look for in stories that could entertain us—a really insightful discussion, and one that helped them focus on the positive results of reading rather than just the mechanics.

As I left the school on the Thursday after Easter, I was reflecting on the enjoyment the smaller kids were gaining from Blinky and pondering how, through the expression with which I read aloud, they might be picking up the real value of punctuation. Mentally, as I walked back to my hoochie on the veranda, I started to rehearse my reading performance.

At Kegworth I had bought totally into the need for a teacher to perform. Teachers, I came to believe, must at times adopt personas, attitudes, behaviours and roles so as to stimulate the children, imbuing lessons with drama and fun—often to revivify flagging interest. I was fully aware that when kids are sitting in one place for up to six hours a day, they become distracted sometimes and, understandably, bored. I accepted that part of my role was to help them through low times with a touch of make-believe. *Handstands in the aisles and swinging from the chandeliers* were my thoughts as I acted out and tried to have as much enjoyment as did the kids.

I strolled slowly along, deep in silent planning, down the school track and then onto the main road. Across that road and just up the hill from my lodgings was the compound of three huts where the elderly brother and sister lived. We'd occasionally waved a greeting to each other, but because they never left their property—as far as I could tell—I had no opportunity to speak with them. From time to time I had pondered if they could gaze straight into my camp on the veranda and know more about me than I would want them to know. Even so, I'd decided to introduce myself to them if an opportunity arose.

That afternoon I noticed the brother in his yard, so I crossed the road, shook hands and gave my name. He introduced himself as Perc Buckland. I could see he was in his late seventies. His sister, he explained, was named Ethel, and he invited me to meet her and take afternoon tea with them. It was already late in the day, almost dark, as was usual when I left the school, so I begged off and said I'd join them the next day.

That following afternoon, Perc showed me around their property before we went in for the refreshments. The first of the three huts, right on the road, was a tumbledown, galvanised-iron affair, its walls leaning in all directions and seemingly dependent on overgrown vines for their ability to stay upright. Perc told me this was where he slept. It had been the petty sessions courthouse in years gone by. I didn't ever see inside.

Perc told me he acted as an agent for a New England hide merchant. Any local with hides, skins, furs or pelts to sell brought them to Perc, and he stored them in his hut until the monthly attendance of the merchant. After the hides were valued, the money was handed over to Perc and could then be distributed to the right people. This kept him in touch with some of the locals, and he chatted happily with them when they visited with hides. Apart from that, neither Perc nor Ethel had any contact with their neighbours as they never ventured beyond their own boundaries.

The second hut, down the slope a little from the first, was a more substantial wooden structure. It was only one small room, though, with a tiny front veranda. This was Ethel's hut, where she had her bedroom. Sometimes, when I later called on the siblings, she would be sitting in a wicker chair on the veranda. I saw inside this hut once only, when she was in bed sick but wanted to say hello. The little room was neat, with lined walls, and Ethel lay in a proper old iron bed with a snowy-white spread. A wardrobe and bedside cabinet quite filled the rest of the space. There was a vase of flowers, some books and magazines on the cabinet, and a rug on the floor. It was snug and gave an air of comfort, although I could see no sign of any fire having been laid in the fireplace.

On my first visit, Perc and I proceeded down the hill a little further, along a well-trodden track, until we came to the third hut, in which the brother and sister did much of their living. Here I met Ethel for the first time. She seemed a year or two younger than her brother but still well into her seventies.

This hut was also of galvanised iron, with not one right-angled corner to be seen. Thick vines covered the walls and roof. There was no window, so sunlight only entered when the door, swung on leather hinges, was left open. It took me some minutes to regain my full vision. The walls were unlined, and the rafters, of rough-cut tree branches, were visible just over-head. The dirt floor was almost level and very clean; decades of use had packed it down hard and smoothed it out, with a little shine from so many footsteps. At one end was a huge open fireplace, but there was no cooking range or stove. Above the fire hung a metal arrangement—a crane, the siblings told me. Its various branches or arms, each at a different height from the hearth, could hold a pot or pan over the flames.

The table had been created by banging two large tree stumps into the earth and then attaching hand-sawn planks on top. I soon discovered any cup or mug had to be placed with care to ensure the contents didn't tip or spill. On each side of the rough table were long stools for sitting, each made from two small tree stumps driven into the earth and the careful placement of roughly cut planks. These had been smoothed out over the decades, so I had no fear of splinters. Beside the fire was a sagging, softly upholstered chair, its stuffing hanging out all over; it was draped with a multi-coloured rug, crocheted by Ethel in years gone by.

Whenever I visited, we'd sit before the fire in this hut. Ethel would take the soft chair, and Perc and I would sit on the stools on opposite sides of the table. Except when Ethel was sick, we never varied that seating pattern over my hundreds of visits.

There was no electricity in Weabonga. In the Bucklands' huts, light was provided by one pressure lamp in the living hut and smaller kerosene lamps to take to each bedside. If we sat talking until it grew dark, we sat on with just the firelight jumping about, illuminating little. There was ease in speaking intimately in the semi-dark.

On my first visit I was stunned by the siblings' living arrangements, but I quickly came to disregard them: my joy in spending time with the elderly pair overrode everything. I paid attention only to our happy chatter and vibrant conversations.

Perc was still strikingly handsome, and Ethel was always alert, lively and merry of face. They got about easily enough, although never with any speed. Their lifestyle had helped them to remain slim, and they stood very upright, with strong handshakes, and bright and open gazes. Both laughed easily and smiled often.

That first afternoon it was love at first sight for me, and it seemed mutual. Perhaps, like me, they were starved of companionship. Perhaps, like me, they revelled in talk of current affairs, politics and society. Perhaps, like me, they loved reading and discussing books. Whatever was in play in our friendship, we never stopped to analyse it, just thoroughly enjoyed it for what it was.

~

After that first visit, I sat with Ethel and Perc several times each week and shared many cups of tea as we discussed the world, our opinions, and our likes and dislikes. In more than seventy years the siblings had never been further from Weabonga than Tamworth, thirty miles away, and neither had any secondary education. But they were wise and insightful and surprisingly well read. After carefully testing out my opinions over a few visits, they began to be more outspoken.

I'd found most people I knew to be progressive in their thinking, and there seemed to be a general agreement that Australia needed to change. Nearly everyone I talked with was concerned about the poor level of educational provision; the lack of good health care and hospitals, particularly in regional areas; and the lack of efficient industries that could compete with those of other developed nations. Australia, to most I knew, seemed an unnecessarily backward country, and we all wanted to see progression. No matter one's political persuasion there was general support for initiative and development. So in that sense I wasn't at all surprised by Perc and Ethel's modern ideas, but I found it remarkable that folk of their age wanted change as desperately as I did.

Australia's involvement in both the Korean War and the Malayan Emergency had been unnecessary and unwise. Ethel and Perc could see trouble brewing in Vietnam and believed our country would be drawn in—and they didn't want that. The ongoing Cold War was a great worry to them.

They believed that Bob Menzies, a prime minister for whom they had never voted, was disappointing, and they found, from their pensioners' point of view, he was hard to trust. We all felt that development should have been receiving significantly greater governmental support. Australia's annual growth rate of just over one per cent was regrettable to all of us at a time when we believed the country should have been booming. And while Perc and Ethel both spoke with a pleasant, lilting accent, they found Menzies' plummy tones a bit silly and affected.

The siblings delivered their opinions with style and humour. Both were witty and often provoked loud laughter. Merriment rippled along under every conversational stream. Both were always interesting, and there was no lull in our chatter. Not once did we look at each other and say that it must be five to the hour as a silence had descended.

From them I heard little of the past, and I admired that, at their ages, their focus was almost entirely on the future. They rarely spoke about their early life and not once referred to their parents. On only one occasion did either comment on the early history of Weabonga: Perc told of the enjoyment he'd received from riding his horse for weeks at a time around a large district to distribute and collect the census papers.

While accepting that the past was forbidden territory, I couldn't help but feel what a treasure they would have been to an oral historian, if they did decide to share their memories. Through a little fossicking in records, I found that the Court of Petty Sessions—of which their father had been the appointed magistrate—had opened in Weabonga, or Swamp Oak as it was known, in 1891, and the magistrate had presided in the courthouse tin shed until his sudden, totally unexpected death. Assuming they'd come to the village with their father in 1891, Ethel and Perc would have been young children on arrival and seen nearly seventy years pass by as village residents.

Ethel told me that once a week Bon brought them, in his mail car, newspapers delivered originally to his home for his family to read during the preceding week. Each paper was read, by Ethel and Perc, from cover to cover in the correct calendar order. They then re-read each, many times over. Bon also brought them any paperbacks he could scrounge, along with recycled magazines that folk along his mail route would hand back on his next run.

They had a radio, tuned mostly to the ABC and listened to for many hours each day. I had not heard them tune to the local radio, which played turgid songs either about faithful dogs or unfaithful lovers.

We spent loads of time discussing books, both past gems and present joys. Whenever I spent time away from Weabonga, I returned with reading materials. Most were for my students, but I also carried back anything I thought my elderly friends might enjoy.

We immersed ourselves in Dickens. I had begun reading fiction early in primary school but it was *Great Expectations*—which

I read when I was about ten and borrowed from the travelling library of Randwick Municipality—that had introduced me to adult novels. That extraordinary scene of the convict rising out of the mud had captured me for all time.

Perc explained that he'd been about the same age as me, about ten years old, when he'd also first read Dickens. The difference being that, for Perc, the novels had been published only thirty or so years earlier but, by the time I was swept up by them, they'd been read and loved for nearly a century. Nevertheless, to both of us they were fresh and remarkable doorways to new experiences.

We all agreed that the opening of *Bleak House*, with the embroiling London fog, was the best piece of descriptive writing any of us had enjoyed. We had all entered unfamiliar worlds through that and other creations of Dickens. The siblings explained this was, among many benefits, a great joy they received from their reading: a good novel could take them away from Weabonga and give them satisfying experiences available to them in no other way.

We all shared a love of Thomas Hardy and could never agree which novel was his best. They chided me on my preference for and love of *Jude the Obscure*.

Perc jibed, 'You like it as you identify with Jude, deprived by circumstances from pursuing further education.'

That struck home, as did Ethel's suggestion. 'No. You like it as it begins with a schoolmaster leaving the village school.'

What prescience. I hadn't revealed my recent decision to seek a transfer if matters didn't improve, so these comments underscored our closeness. Perc and Ethel always seemed to have clear insight into my feelings and concerns, but I never found that disconcerting—rather, it was reaffirming.

Of the American authors, Hemingway and Steinbeck met with our approval, but when I mentioned Salinger there was a silence. Even when, after a holiday in Sydney, I was able to supply a copy of *The Catcher in the Rye*, they couldn't share my unabashed enthusiasm. Perhaps you just had to have read it when you were sixteen to have been struck with wonder at its veracity.

I spoke to them about the books read by, shared around and discussed by all my mates. This included a recount of how, at one point, the six of us had gone through a phase of reading on the beach and enjoying any undemanding, one-shilling paperback Western, especially anything by Louis L'Amour. They giggled a bit at that confession, but when I said we'd all been bowled over by *Atlas Shrugged*, laughter ceased. They had heard this novel and its author discussed on the radio, and remembered some critic's reading of it as fascist propaganda. That forced me to think about it more clearly. From then on, Perc and Ethel made me more aware of the underlying messages in novels I chose to read.

Thinking about *Great Expectations*, as we did occasionally, had me remembering that the heiress in the story had been modelled on an Australian woman, while the convict character had made his fictional fortune from a sheep property in the colony. Maybe that sheep station had been near Weabonga. I thought of the lives of my elderly friends: beginning with much promise then leaving them stranded at a young age, and never suggesting a way to succeed or even to extricate themselves from the trap they were in. Either Hardy or Dickens might have made a compelling novel from these ingredients. Such thoughts, though, I never shared with my pair of dearest companions.

Each time I visited we took part in a minor tea ceremony. Perc and Ethel could observe the school, on its little rise, from their property on the adjacent hill, so they knew the exact moment I commenced my walk to visit them. When I reached their hut the kettle was just on the boil. Taking in hand a hessian square—edged with fabric by Ethel—Perc lifted the kettle from the fire and wet the leaves in the teapot Ethel had waiting. We each took a biscuit—a buttered Sao, or an Anzac cookie baked by Ethel in the camp oven placed directly in the fire—then we were ready for Ethel to pour. No cup matched any saucer, and all crockery was of a similar light brown, whatever its original colouring, the pieces patterned with crazed veins. They were the remnants of any number of tea services going back over seventy years, and to take tea was to hold history in one's hand. A small jar of powdered milk and a sugar bowl with a beaded net cover stood ready on the table. As we performed our ritual, not one moment was wasted. Both brother and sister had a topic ready to set us talking, and away we'd go. With each visit I nestled contentedly into the routine; it was warm, hospitable and calming, and I felt cherished.

I never questioned how it was that my friendship with folk at least fifty years my senior was such an important part of my life. The friendship was never taken for granted, and I thanked the stars, or whatever had overheard me in my darkest times, for gifting me such gorgeous company.

Perc and Ethel, I loved.

12

The children had a marvellous resource for reading practice in *The School Magazine*, published each month by the Education Department in upper and lower primary versions. That journal was already venerable, recognised for its quality and worth in world publishing. Topical, factual articles were accompanied by stories, poems and plays, often composed by well-known, established authors of the time. My pupils loved it; they looked forward to the new copy each month, read it voraciously, and returned to their favourite stories and articles many times over.

Each child had a stiff cardboard folder in which to store their magazines. Loops of string, threaded between the pages, retained all the magazines in the holder over the year. The children would keep these folders always nearby and in every spare moment ferret out their favourites and get busy re-reading.

Prior to distributing each magazine to the children, I made flashcards for those words I knew would be new and maybe problematic. I was ready to assist the kids in gaining greatest enjoyment when they pounced on their copy.

Through the magazines my students increased their word recognition; practised comprehension and reading for meaning; performed the plays; recited the poems as a choral group or as solo performers; solved puzzles—and just enjoyed themselves. Hours of active learning accompanied every edition, and I wrote to let the editor know how much receiving the magazine meant to these isolated pupils.

Apart from the magazine we had little reading material to begin with. Overall the kids enjoyed reading, but I was never convinced they were able to do enough. As their homes lacked electricity, it was hard for them to read at night. I had no expectation that they could, would or should read at home, just as I had no expectation that they would do homework. Most reading for pleasure had to take place at school, so I tried to make space for it. The kids knew that their completion of any tasks ahead of time could be supplemented by some independent reading. As most had no models of reading at home, I wanted to reinforce the usefulness and joy they could obtain from books and other publications. By my gradual building up of the stock of books for reading pleasure, the children were introduced to a range of authors and tales they came to love.

The young ones had departmental readers featuring the characters David, Sue and Wendy, so we worked our way through those. The first of them, *Let's Read*, introduced our youngest pair to reading and had twenty or so words to be learnt by sight. Jimmy could read the entire book by the second day; Charlie, though, took some months to gain faltering mastery over the words. *Seaside Story* followed, which, as the title suggests, contained content totally unfamiliar to the kids; neither had seen the sea, let alone built castles on the golden sands. *Open Road to Reading*, the third instalment, was based around a family with a father who set off each day to the office in his suit, tie and snappy hat, with his briefcase. It took much explaining to Charlie and Jimmy for them to begin to gain any understanding of such a lifestyle.

Rather than leaving the young ones to flounder with stories for which they lacked any context, we decided once more to write our own. Producing the simple 'up' and 'down' stories had excited Charlie and Jimmy.

Finding content was easy: each Monday morning the kids reported news items that provided lots of ideas for exciting material. Memorable was a discussion of the word 'slithering', which the children had suggested we use in the written-down story of Lindie's snake-in-a-pantry thriller. Susie said she loved the word and enjoyed another one in the story: 'hissing'.

When asked to explain, Carol gradually got out, 'Each word sounds like it should, and each has a pattern that looks like it should.'

It was Rick—one of the village boys, all close observers of nature—who said, '"Slithering" is a long, low word, except it has three curves where the snake is coiling.'

And it was quick-witted Susie, again, who said, '"Hissing" is also a long, low word, with the fangs out to begin and end, but you have to be a snake to say the word.'

'Yes,' cried all the others as they *hiiissssed* and *hiiiissssed*.

Some words are onomatopoeic, and the children grasped that concept easily enough that day. No child ever stumbled over 'slithering' or 'hissing' when the word occurred in later reading.

Gradually, by documenting such stories, we accumulated a stock of readers better suited to the kids. All loved the books they had jointly written and engaged wholeheartedly in contributing the illustrations.

Tom and Jack recounted a lengthy tale of a camping trip they had undertaken on horseback one weekend. They'd left Tom's homestead on the Saturday morning and ridden for five hours due west through wild, uncharted, heavily timbered country. The boys had known that if they kept westward they would eventually reach Duffys Creek and find, on its downstream banks, an isolated shearing shed where they could shelter for the night. Both asserted their confidence they wouldn't lose their way. The other kids, their listeners, were convinced of this too; the two older boys were models for proper male behaviour in the eyes of all.

Tom and Jack's riding and camping story reminded us of the distinctly Australian anxiety about children being lost in the bush. Early in February, just after I'd commenced at the school, the children had chattered about a little boy who had been lost outside the town of Guyra, also in New England and not that far as the crow flies from our school. The search for the child kept the kids talking for many days, and we all cheered when news came of him being found and rescued. A little later the children started singing a song about the boy, one they'd heard on the radio; after reaching number one on the local station's hit parade, it became as well known as the lost boy himself.

Jack and Tom told us they had, indeed, lost their direction once during their camping trip, but felt no real concern. Both were confident of their bushman skills, and they'd reoriented themselves after breaking clear of some heavy scrub and sighting the Sugarloaf, a mountain south-west of the village.

We all worked together to write out a version of this story, which was titled by agreement 'Two Mates', and Tom produced a marvellous set of pen-and-ink sketches to illustrate the important elements from his and Jack's point of view. All the children loved to read this story, whether in Grade One or Five, the littlies being helped to read by the older students.

Young Charlie offered his own story one Monday. I held my breath, hoping for a triumph but ready to offer assistance if necessary. The episode was most memorable, as Charlie was unusually assertive. This was his breakthrough performance. His brothers attempted to prompt him as he spoke, but he was having none of it. Haltingly, but with a positive trajectory despite his shyness, he delivered his tale.

'Last Saturday my dad got lots of old metal bits together. He had rusty bits of barbed wire and he had broken bits of corrugated iron and he had old tins with holes and that, and he threw these in our ute and then he got me, Phil and Mike in the ute and then he drove down the Limbri Road a bit and then he took a track off into the bush and then he stopped when we came to an old mine.'

At about this point Mike, Charlie's older brother, tried to intervene to tell us all which mine and where the shaft was located. But Charlie wouldn't accept being overtaken. He said, very firmly, 'I'm telling this news.' He went on, 'Dad wouldn't let me get out but I could see Dad and Phil and Mike take the old stuff off the back and throw it bit by bit down the mine hole, but I was frightened that Dad or them might fall down the hole and I was happy when the job was done and I was happy that I had worked with Dad and I was happy we had got the job done really well and I felt real good. Dad said he was pleased with me and me brothers.'

Charlie helped develop this story into a written and illustrated booklet, contributing some colourful pictures. He included, with prompts from the other children, that the Highland Mary, where the rubbish had been tipped, was the long-disused shaft of the biggest, richest-producing and last-closed of the district's goldmines.

Charlie learnt quickly to sight-read the story and even enjoyed reading it aloud to the others. They loved to hear him, gave great encouragement each time and heaped praise when he had it fully read. He glowed when he was the centre of attention.

Until that day, Charlie's shoebox had contained only about sixty sight words; after, he added new words nearly every day until he needed an extra box. Soon he had a collection of many hundreds of sight words and was on his way to being an independent reader. Having long doubted that outcome, I took immense pleasure in Charlie's success.

From Vickie, Mark and Carol Thomas, whose home was secreted in the bush on the opposite bank of the creek, we heard an appealing story. The three of them batted the narrative back and forth.

Vickie commenced, so very quietly we all strained to hear. 'We have a new rooster. I didn't like him at first. When I went into the yard he used to fly at me. I was afraid of his spurs. I thought he could hurt me.'

Mark continued, 'He's a big, red fellow. We call him Rusty. He's only young. Dad said, "Don't you worry about him," but we were afraid.'

Carol chimed in, 'Even Mum wouldn't go near him. When we had to get the eggs, she stood near us. She wouldn't let Rusty come close to us.'

And so the story grew.

'Dad told us Rusty was just doing what he had to do. Dad said Rusty thought he was the boss. He was keeping the chooks safe. Dad said Rusty would learn we wouldn't harm any of the fowls. Then he'd stop going for us.'

'So we kept the best veggie scraps for Rusty. We gave them to him when the other chooks were already locked up for the night.'

'Rusty loved the green scraps. He'd gobble them all up. He comes when we call him now—he knows us.'

'Now we love Rusty. He even sits on our lap for a petting sometimes.'

'All the chooks have names and they know their pet name. Rusty always comes if we call, "Rusty, Rusty."'

'Dad says Rusty is the best rooster we've ever had. Mum likes him now. She says Rusty is a brave, strong rooster.'

What a delight it was for the kids to write up and illustrate that story. The schoolroom walls were decorated with wonderful drawings and paintings of scarlet and ruby-red birds with huge feathers, breast-deep in emerald-tinted vegie scraps, for more than a week. Some of the depictions brilliantly caught the rooster's evil-looking yellow eye.

13

The weekend after my first meeting with Ethel and Perc, at the Sunday afternoon tennis party, a fellow around my age introduced himself as Paul Williamson. He'd never been to the tennis before but told me he knew from gossip that I attended each Sunday, and he'd come just to meet and talk with me. Paul was from the third sheep property along the Limbri Road, only a little over three miles from the village, but I'd never seen him before.

Our talk was mainly about rugby. Was I a player? Was I thinking of joining a team for the upcoming season? I answered that I'd have liked to, but explained I had no car. That was no trouble to my new friend. He would pick me up on the coming Saturday morning, take me to town and help me sign up to the Tamworth Rugby Union Club. So, I now had something to look forward to.

The busy week passed quickly. From my veranda camp on the Saturday, I saw Paul's car pull up. On getting in, I was introduced to my friend's father, George Williamson, a chap in his eighties. They were in a classic Holden ute, so we three sat side by side across the bench seat. We chatted as we drove, about an hour into Tamworth. All of us had shopping to do, so we dispersed then met up again at the Tudor Hotel in the main street. We had a drink and a quick lunch in the upstairs bar, which was to become my favourite spot in the town.

After lunch, we drove George to visit one of his married daughters, Joan, who lived in West Tamworth. There were four daughters: Joan, married in Tamworth; Margaret, married and living on a property near Rowena in the Pilliga Scrub; and two yet unmarried, Elizabeth and Barbara, who were both practising nurses.

After dropping his dad off, my new friend and I continued on to the rugby club in a side street across town. As it was registration day there were many would-be players, and the afternoon became a chatty time. Introductions were made, new friendships commenced, and old friendships fired up. I met forty or so people. They were especially approachable, enjoyable company, and I felt relaxed and hopeful that any future with this lively group could only be pleasant.

The club was to field two teams in the regional rugby competition, so it needed every one of the players who came to register that day. With fifteen a side and a couple of reserves, the club needed a representation of at least thirty-four players each Saturday. Clubs were also expected to supply some officials, especially sideline judges, for each game. Accounting for expected injuries and winter sickness, a forty-strong playing group would just about cover the necessary numbers.

The competition included some of the larger towns in the north and north-west of the state, so during the season we would travel for games at Narrabri, Armidale, Walcha, Gunnedah and Quirindi. This would give me the chance to meet numbers of convivial country folk from all these centres.

Later in the afternoon on registration day, groups of young women began to arrive at the clubhouse: the girlfriends and wives of the players. The club had a bar serviced by volunteers, although there wasn't much drinking as many players lived out of town on farm properties and had to drive home. Socialising was the norm after training or after any game, and later I learnt that a small orchestra might be brought in for dancing. But that day the entertainment was supplied by the members present.

As is well known, rugby has lots of songs, many ribald but all fun, which all players can sing, whatever the quality of their voice. Among the group present were some who had excellent voices, and they led the singing, encouraging everyone to join in. Later in the year, I attended musical theatre produced by the Tamworth Amateur Theatrical Society to hear the good rugby club singers in quite demanding roles. Sometimes I wished I'd been located closer to the town so that I could have auditioned for a role in these productions. Singing had always been a normal and expected part of my life, and I enjoyed singing in a group, so the rugby club, that first day, was almost like coming home—lots of music, lots of songs, lots of young people enjoying themselves.

One song I heard for the first time that registration day I found bemusing. A group of guys started softly but increased the volume as they got into the song, first tapping out then stamping out the rhythm. The song concerned New England—lots of stress on that—and its seeking of separation from New South Wales. Words that came through included 'rousing', 'marching', 'fight', 'battle cry', 'liberty'. It was a call for statehood: 'We will raise the banner of New England.' I thought the song humorous and satirical, and was later much surprised when others spoke to me of the serious intention of some folk to raise the standard and fight for New England, a new state. *How extraordinary*, I thought.

On our way back to Weabonga, George and Paul questioned me about my living arrangements and listened quietly to my responses. I held back a bit as I didn't know how close they might be to the O'Callaghans, and I didn't want to seem too critical of the only family who would take me in.

George asked if I'd like to spend the night and next day visiting with his family on their farm property. Through politeness I suggested I might not, hoping my response would be dismissed. It was, and so we continued through the village to their homestead, just off the Limbri Road.

It was so late when we arrived that there was only just time for me to meet Barbara. She was one of the two unmarried daughters, a qualified nurse, off work and staying at home to care for her elderly father and run the household.

My bed was comfortable, with a soft mattress and feather-stuffed quilt spread. In the morning I was shown how to light the chip heater so I could shower and shave with hot water in a fully equipped bathroom. Breakfast was served by Barbara at a table set up on a side veranda, which overlooked a small house paddock through an autumnal Virginia creeper; beyond the paddock was the Swamp Oak Creek, lined with she-oaks. We ate fresh scrambled eggs from the chooks that scratched around in the adjoining field, with lots of toast and pats of butter from the Jersey cow giving us the eye and occasionally mooing through the fence. Marmalade and blackberry jam were on offer, made last season by our hostess.

After we'd eaten, while we enjoyed our second or third cup of tea, Paul said the family had something to propose for my consideration. I didn't really know what to expect.

George said, 'Peter, we've been thinking, and we'd like to suggest you come and live with us here for the remainder of your stay in Weabonga.'

I couldn't restrain myself. 'Yes, yes! Of course. How wonderful of you to offer. Of course. I'd be over the moon. How marvellous.' But I then backtracked, 'Are you all sure? Do you all want that? It would be wonderful for me but I don't want to put you out in any way. Are you certain?'

Paul said, 'No worries, we all agree. We wouldn't have made the offer if it wasn't genuinely meant. We'd be very happy for you to live here.'

Barbara added, 'We discussed it while you were showering, and it's a unanimous decision. Please come to live here with us.'

I confirmed my acceptance and thanked them as whole-heartedly as I had ever given thanks in my life. The stars, from whatever friendly galaxy, had again truly shone their light on me that morning.

Later in the day, Paul drove me back to the village to gather my things, give my thanks and say goodbye to my landlords. These farewells weren't easy, and I didn't want them to feel I was rejecting them. Of course I was doing just that, and there was really no way to soften my message.

I didn't blame Lawrie and Jill. After a while I'd come to understand more about and empathise with their difficult, rather hand-to-mouth existence. I'd grown to appreciate the fact they had taken me in at all. Jill, in particular, had tried to do what she could to make my life easier—it was just that she had so little with which to work. The family ate much the same as I did, and I felt a concern for them. Lawrie took whatever work he could, but it was obvious most of his employment was with his dad, and many of his siblings had to be supported from the one income the family's small property might derive. How significant my monthly cheque had been to the household finances couldn't be hidden.

I'd also come to appreciate that the O'Callaghans desperately wanted their boys to receive an education. Without their accommodation there would have been no school, and I would never have come to Weabonga.

Packing was easy and quick: I just had to shut the lid of my suitcase and take off.

⌒

Patricia was very relieved for me when I told her of my changed circumstances in our next phone call. She'd also recently established better, longer-term accommodation by moving into a

South Yarra share flat with two young women, both of them likeable and reliable, and they'd all settled in well.

Patricia told me that one flatmate's job gave her access to food supplies meant for TV production crews, and she would sometimes bring home leftovers to share.

'Dining on two Sargents pies each isn't sophisticated but saves us money and work. We might have a glass of white and pretend and have a good laugh.'

Yes, I thought, *when you're young you just have to make do.*

14

The NSW curriculum included arts and crafts, music and dance, science, and physical activities to ensure the children were healthy. As my pupils lived in a remote spot, I wanted them to experience the widest range of subjects and activities possible. Each curriculum area was important in its own right, and none would be neglected by me. I also believed that a child's weaker performance in one area might be balanced with a stronger performance in another. I wanted all the children to experience success and to form a belief that they could do well in some areas of learning—all of them deserved to see themselves as competent.

The children were already scientists. If observation is the bedrock upon which science is based, then at Weabonga we had a whole laboratory of eager experimenters. As country kids they looked around constantly for the signs and warnings of what might happen in their environment, and they had a sharp understanding of their surroundings.

All could read the clouds. Following a schoolyard break they would tell me, quite accurately, the weather the next few hours would bring. As I passed them by in the village on my way home, one might yell, 'You'll be jake, Sir. It won't rain for an hour or two.'

Snow in the village wasn't frequent, but the children were accurate forecasters. 'See the green in that cloud over the Sugarloaf?' they'd say to each other, pointing to the sky. 'It'll be snowing like billy-oh in a tick.' And the sky would glower a dirty khaki, and snow it would.

So we learnt the names of all cloud types. We drew cloud-scapes and kept rainfall records. We averaged out rainfall over days of the month.

Natural sciences were natural to the kids, so we did much careful observation of the bush around us. We enjoyed nature rambles, with my pupils tramping along, roughly together. On one autumn trek, a hot little hand slipped into mine. Generally I didn't promote or accept such familiarity, but when I looked down and saw it was Charlie, our littlest, I held the hand softly.

As we walked, Charlie said, 'Native apple.'

Nothing further.

I let it ride for a few seconds then asked, 'Where, Charlie? I'm not great at recognising trees so you'll have to help me. Which one is a native apple?'

He nodded and pointed his free hand in the direction of a copse. 'There. That one.'

'Good-oh, but there are several different trees in that group. How do I know the native apple?'

'Easy,' replied Charlie, with a hint of exasperation, 'you look at the colour because all the others are all grey and the native apple is the greeny one and the native apple's branches go out straight from the tree, they don't grow up only, they all grow sideways. It's easy to tell. Trees look different.'

That was the longest one-on-one communication I'd ever enjoyed with Charlie. I pressed his small hand. 'Thanks, Charlie. You've taught me something important.'

We exchanged a smile: one of Charlie's delightful, warming expressions.

I soon included physics in our studies. When I introduced the concept of a lever, Will immediately went to an example, citing an experience with his dad and a green tree. Will's dad was Max Baulderstone, one of the Sunday tennis players.

'What do you mean, Will?' I asked. 'A green tree? Please tell us more.'

'Okay,' he said. 'One day a few months back Dad took me and Gary in our ute to the McCreas' farm up on the Niangala Road. He was dropping off some gravel to the McCreas.'

'Oh, yeah,' Will's brother Gary chimed in, 'I remember that.'

'On our way back home, the ute had a flat. Dad said a bad word and told us he didn't have the car jack in the back. He said he'd taken it out of the ute to carry the gravel and had forgotten to put it back in.'

'Yeah,' offered Gary, 'it was a real bad word. We're not allowed to say it so we said to Dad we'd tell Mum.'

'Dad said fair cop but told us not to worry. "I can fix this," he said.'

Max had found a young, green eucalypt, fairly tall but slim. Gary explained: 'Dad told us it couldn't be a dead branch as that'd snap under a ute's weight.'

Their dad shimmied up the thin tree to the very top and, with his body mass on it, bent it to the ground. By pressing and forcing and jumping on it close to the base, he eventually broke the stem. He now had a long pole.

'Dad told us, "Okay, boys, collect a couple of big rocks, flat as possible."'

These rocks were packed carefully under the appropriate axle, and Max introduced one end of the tree trunk under the ute.

'Dad called out, "Stand clear."'

Making sure everything was stable, Max swung his weight on the furthest end of the tree trunk and raised the car from the roadway.

'Dad told us, "Now, you fellers hop on here and hang your weight on the end of the tree. Here, where it's low to the ground. But, for gosh-sakes, be very careful. If you feel the branch move just let it go and run like hell out of the way."'

I was hoping Max had crossed more than his fingers, as I listened in trepidation.

The boys said they'd reassured Max. 'Okay, Dad. We know what to do.'

Their combined weight was enough to keep the car raised, and Max effected the wheel replacement. The car was let down under his supervision, tree and rocks removed, and the trio continued on their way home.

'Wonderful, Gary and Will, and so well told,' I responded. 'We were all really anxious from your retelling to know what happened.' Then I asked the inevitable teacher-type question. 'Now, everybody, what name could we give to the green tree trunk when their dad made it lift the car?'

'It was a lever,' most called.

'And, what was the fulcrum?'

'The rocks stacked up under the axle,' called out Joe Wallace.

'Well understood and correct, Joe,' was his reward.

While appreciating the spontaneous bush ingenuity of Max's solution, I was startled by the inherent danger for him and especially for the two boys. But I chose not to comment that morning on safety.

A week or so later we picked up a focus on the care the children needed to exercise around farms. Farm work, I knew from reports in the *Northern Daily Leader*, was among the most injury-prone and dangerous of occupations—and, from the boys' telling, I could see why. But that day we continued with stories referring to a lever.

Mike, who often visited his grandfather Cyril O'Callaghan's property and helped with farm jobs, spoke out: 'Just like a wool press.'

'How, Mike?'

'Well, a wool press has a long handle, and the presser pushes that handle down, and the handle presses down on the wool. And the pressing can be so strong that a lot of wool can be pressed down to a fairly small pile, which you can pin up to make a bale.'

'Absolutely correct, Mike. Well done. What do we call the long handle on the wool press?'

'It's a lever,' the children responded, with a bit of a giggle. They seemed to love the fact that a simple piece of familiar, everyday machinery included something with a formal, even scientific name.

15

In my joy at moving into the Williamson homestead, I didn't consider transport arrangements. What I quickly came to regard as my home lay about three miles along the Limbri Road from the village, so the question of travel was an important one. I wasn't at all worried about walking each way although, as it turned out, I walked only occasionally. Being young and reasonably fit, and wanting to be even fitter as the football season approached, I knew any required walking would be sensible. If Paul had completed his paddock work when I arrived back at the homestead in the late afternoon, we would sometimes run together for a few miles up the road and back: our attempts at gaining fitness for our Saturday matches.

There were many times, though, when I would have to carry piles of books or large items for instructional purposes. And the walk would take up to an hour each way—time I preferred to use in other ways. In winter, which was approaching when I moved, walking could also mean leaving and arriving home in the dark, while traversing a rocky, uneven road lit only by the moon and stars.

But when I did walk I savoured the experience. The road ran along the creek, and green fields lay on either side, smoothed by the grazing of stock. The stream-side paddocks had been cleared maybe eighty years earlier, and there were scattered stumps of eucalypts that must have once been considerably tall and wide. They had been felled to create pasture or to harvest mine props, but there was no feeling of degradation at any step in my journey. Scattered trees had been spared, and on hotter days sheep and cattle sheltered in deep shadows.

In the mornings the air was sweet with the faint smell of creek water and the scent of decaying she-oak needles. Sometimes a pair of goannas, residents in a field at one road bend, took off in fright at the sight of me. If I spotted them just as they spotted me, I'd see them rear up by straightening their front legs; they then stood at least waist high. Off they would crash, breaking down bushes and woody weeds in their thunderous flight. But usually the walk to school was relaxing and encouraged easeful thoughts, while giving me time to polish my plans for the day.

The late-afternoon walk home could be especially appealing. At midday the colours of the bush would be dulled and washed out, showing drab olives and greys, but later in the day the quality of the light would soften and become almost golden, and then the bush was luminous, its hidden colours beginning to show. The heights of the surrounding hills, with the sun's rays hitting them obliquely, glowed copper and gold. As I ambled along I would notice a spot of pink here, a dash of orange there, a splotch of light blue in a gum branch, and a score or more shades of green in the vegetation. Rocks no longer showed a monotonous dark grey: specks of mica shone, drops of silver and red stood out, white emerged in places. Smells sharpened, eucalypt merging with wattle and briar rose. Native thyme and myrtle scented the corners already in shadow. The creek was trickling and bubbling over its rocky bed, and I could better detect the metallic taint of the water; it had a distinctive odour, more noticeable in the cooler evenings. Birds, in their scurry just prior to dark descending, would chirp, whistle, call or coo. A slight evening breeze might ruffle the grasses, and I could almost see the wind as it lifted the leaves, the smaller branches, then the crowns of the apples, gums and box. I came to revel in the bush.

One of the school families, the Wallaces, lived a number of farm properties further along the Limbri Road than my new home, and they drove their two boys, Joe and Jimmy, to and from school each day. The driving was done almost exclusively by the boys' mother, Marie.

My shift in accommodation was newsworthy and seemed to be known to everyone soon after I made the change—the old party phone trick, I reckoned. It was no surprise, then, when Marie Wallace spoke to me outside the school and offered to pick me up each morning as she passed by the Williamsons' gate. I gratefully accepted the lift, although I knew I'd have to keep walking home each afternoon after staying to prepare the blackboard and lessons.

Our arrangement began well enough. I was always ready on time, waiting at the side of the road outside the gate to the property. Marie was always pleasant, and Joe and Jimmy, who knew me by now, would sometimes tell me about happenings at home the night before. These trips were breezy and congenial.

Only one small matter disconcerted me: lying along the dash was always a powerful, loaded rifle. My seat was in the front, next to Marie as she drove, so the rifle was central to my view. I noted the safety was always on, but I still found the rifle's presence off-putting. Being unused to guns, I worried about vehicles, loaded weapons and children in close proximity. All the locals carried guns in their cars, but I didn't know if these were usually loaded. Paul carried an unloaded rifle under the seat of his Holden ute, with the bullets always kept separately in the glove box.

As I settled in to the lift arrangements, I came to worry less about the rifle. Then, one morning, Marie spotted a large red kangaroo on the roadside above the Swamp Oak Creek. The roo didn't move as we drove past, so she stopped the car and reached for the gun, murmuring about food for the station dogs. The roo was on the passenger side, so Marie trained the rifle straight across my chest above my lap, sighting the target through the open window. I drew my breath as sharply as I was able—if I could have made myself thinner, I would have given it a go.

Having lined up the shot, Marie pulled the trigger. *Bang.*

It took us all a little time to recover our senses. Then we realised the noise hadn't simply been the rifle percussion: right through the passenger door, just above my knees, was a perfectly round hole. Outside, on the road verge, were bits of metal and glass.

Joe and Jimmy began laughing and making fun of their mother. She was a great shot—she could hit any door from any distance. Not quite a barn door this time but, to the boys, a much better one.

The roo, probably relieved, had already hopped off over the creek and up the hill. He'd lived to see another day, but—if I kept getting these lifts—would I?

Soon after this episode I spent the May school holidays in Sydney, socialising with family and friends, especially Patricia.

I made enquiries and finally purchased a second-hand BSA Bantam motorcycle. It wasn't only Marie's Calamity Jane performance that had persuaded me: I needed more flexibility in how and when I travelled. With only a 125cc motor, this small machine was just going to be a handy ride between the Williamsons' and school—I had no intention of travelling any further on it or going anywhere at speed. I'd never ridden a motorbike but signed for a provisional licence that allowed me to begin riding directly after it was delivered by rail and the Limbri mailman, on the back of his utility, to the farm. My first attempt was tentative, but I soon found it was only a little harder than controlling a pushbike. The quicker trips freed up time for school preparation, and now I could spend as much time with Ethel and Perc as I wished, with no worry of walking home three miles in the dark.

Winter came on soon after I began to ride, and some days were bitterly cold. Two sets of gloves, leather layered over wool, couldn't save my hands from freezing, although I was riding only three miles. I had to rub my hands under running water to begin the thawing-out process, which could take ten minutes or more.

On such days the winds whistled and the schoolroom windows rattled in their frames. Once my hands were capable of action I stoked up the Broadway stove in the corner, making the room warm and snug to welcome the children. As they arrived, they hung their jackets and caps on the pegs at the door; on adjacent pegs went their beanies, scarves, gloves and, sometimes, extra jumpers or cardies, all hand-knitted by their mums.

How happy they seemed on those frosty, bright days. They came huffing and puffing through the door, hurried along by the winds biting at any exposed skin and buffeting their eyes. Their cheeks blushed a rosy pink and their eyes sparkled; tears forced by the icy blasts gave each eye a brightness but proved only a temporary problem as the children warmed up. To see them so fresh and eager always lifted my spirits.

The schoolroom, on those winter days, was our sanctuary. The children seemed closer to each other, and I also enjoyed the feelings of nearness and togetherness. We all felt comforted by being safe and warm inside.

16

By our second term together, I'd come to know the children well. Changes in their behaviour still often surprised me, but each child was distinguished by strong characteristics that allowed me to recognise their individuality. Because I took my instructional cues from the children, I had to pay each of them the closest attention.

Tom, now fourteen, was a born leader. Every other student adored him; if he chose to suggest any game or pastime, all the kids readily followed. He was considerate and didn't, in any sense, abuse the position granted him by the younger ones—and they followed him all the more eagerly for that. He'd always been a source of soundness and stability within our group, and he provided a model of sensible behaviour. He chose to support any suggestion of mine and was a reliable back-up if I called on him. He volunteered to assist the younger children by listening to them read, running flashcard activities and reading aloud favourite stories. I had no doubt much of the calm, purposeful and happy air in our school was directly attributable to him. Although he didn't take part in many class activities as a fellow pupil, he was an integral part of the student body. And he loved all of our singing, reciting and acting, so he happily joined in when he chose.

Each week Tom received a bundle of work to be completed and mailed back to his correspondence school in Sydney. Every Monday he settled in quickly and worked consistently, with concentration, at all tasks. They were designed to be self-explanatory, and our teenager was able, with very little assistance from me, to address and complete them. Usually by late Wednesday afternoon Tom would finish all the work set for the week and seek out other activities. His faraway teachers always gave him top marks.

I would have been happy for Tom to have missed school altogether some days. At home he was also successful at all the tasks asked of him and many more he volunteered to do. Modelling himself on his many older brothers, all men with the multiple skills needed in farming, he was already capable in most tasks required in the running of a sheep station. He was valuable at home, and I would have been supportive of him remaining there at times to keep learning farm work and to help his family. He, however, wanted to be at school for the entire week. He loved art, particularly drawing. Some days, having completed his set lessons, he chose to sketch elaborate farm scenes. At a staffed town high school with specialist art teachers, he may well have been able to develop this skill. All I could do was encourage him with art books I'd found in Sydney.

I also gave Tom access to plenty of current rural newspapers, which I brought back from Tamworth. He was avidly interested in reading about all things agricultural, and he discussed articles and viewpoints with me when we had the chance. Lunchtimes might be spent with the two of us on the school veranda, watching the kids at play while Tom nutted out some concepts and used me as a sounding-board.

When Tom mentioned his future, he usually said he'd be a shearer, although he had a major, longer-term ambition to be an independent landowner. Some of his older brothers were in shearing teams that travelled to properties in the west of the state and were away for long stretches. Tom said he was happy to join in that life as it would give him a good income and a chance to save for a deposit on a property of his own.

I could see Tom as a shearing contractor, running big teams of shearers and attracting solid support from graziers. Or perhaps, I thought, he could be a wool classer or surveyor, with some professional qualifications but fulfilling his plan to work outdoors. I couldn't see him, though, having the advantage of further formal education. He wanted to be employed and to leave school when he completed his Intermediate Certificate, after turning fifteen. No doubt he would have been successful proceeding to his Leaving Certificate in a high school, then on to tertiary study at an agricultural college. But his ambitions were formed by his life experiences, and to say those were limiting his vision is just to acknowledge the realities for a boy growing up in an isolated rural area. Additionally, his father would only support him to stay at school until he was fifteen.

The eldest primary children were our four Grade Fives, a gang of three girls and a boy.

Debbie, Tom's little sister, was an aunt to Mike, Phil and Charlie O'Callaghan. She was similar to her brother in many ways: she had the same stocky shape, and was just as quiet and calm. Also like Tom, she carried herself with an upright posture and gave the appearance of strength, even though she was only eleven.

Debbie had instinctive motherly qualities and gave wonderful support to the younger kids, in whose progress she was interested. With her two female classmates, Vickie and Lindie, she had strong friendships and spent a lot of time chatting. She was a joiner, not a leader.

Academically, Debbie performed all tasks in a reasonable manner, and I had no concerns for her development. She was an able reader but might just as easily choose to do craft work. She told me she saw herself in later life as a mother, caring for a home and family. I'd no doubt she would be a very successful mum, but I also thought she would have made a fine nurse or paramedic or any of such health occupations open to women.

Vickie and Lindie were opposites. Vickie was tall, very fair and willowy, while Lindie was shorter, darker and chubby. Vickie was an introvert, quiet and reserved, while Lindie was the most extroverted of all the kids, noisy and quick in all she did. Vickie needed considerable input from me to maintain academic progress, while Lindie mastered most goals with relative ease. Vickie I never heard laugh aloud—although, on occasion, the most appealing subdued titter would break through her natural reserve. Lindie, though, was quite capable of a real guffaw, giggled a lot and almost always presented a lively countenance to her mates.

When talking quietly with me, Vickie spoke of her happiness in spending time just with her mum as they carried out household tasks. Vickie knitted and sewed, crocheted and cooked, practising all the usual feminine skills of the time. She and her mother, Molly, also did some more unusual craft activities, such as soap-, quilt- and rug-making. Their home was almost buried in the bush and quite separate from the others. I gathered the family spent a lot of time in each other's company, seldom venturing out. They never attended the tennis parties, and I can recall seeing Molly on only one occasion apart from the times she attended school functions with her husband. I seldom saw Vickie's father, Dan, in the village and never in conversation with the other men.

The more outgoing Lindie came from a sheep property, but she wasn't isolated. Her father, Vic, was a lay preacher ministering to a circle of rural churches, so she often spoke of Sunday trips away from home where she met people outside the Weabonga community. Lindie enjoyed these outings and would include them in her stories during written composition periods. She was eager for new challenges and would react positively to suggestions made by me or her classmates.

These three Grade Five girls spent time together at recess and lunch, although they often joined in games with the others. They were happy together but never exclusive, and their male classmate, Jack, was always totally accepted as part of their group in the schoolroom. They supported each other in lessons, and seldom gave me cause to suggest they might get back to work and keep the chitchat for a later time.

Jack still chose to sit slightly away from the three girls with his desk alongside theirs. My initial concern that he might become isolated was never realised, as he was always chatting with the others about lessons and schoolwork. When I spent time instructing their grade, Jack would sit alongside one of the girls so that I could speak to them quietly and avoid distracting the others, but he would return quickly to his own desk.

Jack seemed significantly more mature than the Grade Four boys, who were only a year younger. He was more composed, more focused at times, more likely to think before acting and less spontaneous, all qualities that assisted him with academic activities.

Jack had struck up a good friendship with Tom, and they often spent time together at recess and lunch. Sometimes on weekends they'd go camping, just the two of them; they'd ride out into the wilderness, as they described for us a few times. But at school Jack was just as likely to kick a ball around with the younger group as he was to talk to the teenager.

However, although Jack socialised well, there was a slight air of disconnection about him that had contributed to my first apprehension that he might become isolated. I continued to carry a small concern, my mind quietly insisting that as a teacher I should be especially attentive to Jack and mindful of his needs.

One afternoon when I called in to the post office to make a phone call, I was surprised to find an older man serving: it had always before been Sue, Jack and Steve's mum, who'd attended at the counter.

I'd met the older chap only once previously and then just briefly after the one Sunday mass I'd attended at the little Catholic chapel, so he reminded me of his name. 'I'm Tim Bourke,' he coached, 'but call me Tim—always just Tim.'

To have come across a village resident just twice in six months was illustrative, I thought, of the lack of contact between the locals. If folk didn't attend the Sunday tennis, I was unlikely to have seen them. How disconcerting to be isolated from fellow residents in an already isolated village.

I judged Tim to be in his early seventies. We got to talking, and he explained he'd been the postmaster since the 1940s but his daughter, Sue, now managed the PO, as he was retired.

Weeks later, when I came across Tim at the PO once again and we got to chatting companionably, he told me more about his family. 'Jack and Steve's father, David, has separated from Sue. He lives somewhere around the north of the state but he's not in contact with the boys. They haven't seen or spent any time with their dad for more than a year. I opened up my house for my daughter and grandkids. They've made their home with me, and I love having them. I was quite lonely on my own.' The boys, from what I observed, had a close and comfortable relationship with their grandad.

Tim and I got along well, and sometimes we'd sit together on the PO veranda in the late afternoon, sharing a warm bottle of beer while we spoke. I got used to unchilled beer but never developed a liking for it, although the retired postmaster said he preferred it.

During one conversation, he divulged that, 'Dave, the boys' father, is an Aborigine.'

Both boys were fair and resembled their mother, and it hadn't been at all obvious to me they had Aboriginal heritage. I silently reflected that most white people found something a bit shocking about a white woman having kids with an Aboriginal man, and I remembered efforts I'd seen people make to downplay the Aboriginal antecedents of a child. I was familiar with chatter about 'half-castes' and 'quarter-castes', and such children were often pejoratively dubbed 'tar babies' or said to have 'a touch of the tar'.

Sue never spoke to me about the boys' father, so I learnt nothing further.

Casual racism and xenophobia were common and all around me. All my life, outside of my home, I'd heard derogatory and dismissive terms being freely used. New migrants, for example, were called 'reffos' or 'wogs', and mocked for behaviour such as carrying lunch in a briefcase to a labouring job.

Racism was blatantly directed against Aboriginal people, whom whites often referred to as 'blacks', 'abos' or 'boongs'. Aborigines weren't even counted in any census of Australian citizens: officially they weren't considered people fit to be registered by the government. In such circumstances it didn't surprise me that my fellow white Australians frequently exhibited racism with an easy-going, off-hand, flippant attitude. For many of them, Indigenous people weren't quite human but lesser beings.

A lesson I learnt at the age of eleven has stayed with me always. When I commenced high school, I travelled each day from my Kensington home to the Marist Brothers college in Darlinghurst, by tram along Anzac Parade. My stop was on the lines that ran to Maroubra and La Perouse, and sometimes Aboriginal people from the La Perouse community were passengers.

One afternoon, at Taylor Square in Darlinghurst, I began to board a La Perouse tram to travel home. It was an older-style 'toast rack' carriage, with many doors. Adults in front of me were stepping into a compartment—and then, suddenly, they backed out and scurried to another entry. I continued to board. In that compartment, the truth struck me: Aboriginal people were seated there, and the white adults had chosen, very deliberately, not to sit with them.

I can still remember the shock and distress that overcame me as an eleven-year-old. For the first time, I realised that adults couldn't always be trusted to act in the best interests of others. Suddenly and powerfully I knew that adults could be dangerous. Nothing in my home or my schooling had prepared me for this lesson in racism. It was a turning point in my life and, perhaps, the beginning of my growth towards mature understanding. But even at that young age, I knew what I'd seen was wrong and could never be accepted. Racism was inexplicable and abhorrent to my eleven-year-old conscience and has remained despicable to me always.

On some quiet Sundays my mother would take my brother, sister and me on an excursion by tram to La Perouse. There, the Aboriginal snake pit man would be in action, revealing and handling a variety of black, brown and tiger snakes as well as many death adders. Other Aboriginal people would be selling arts and crafts: everything from shell Harbour Bridges and slippers to finely engraved boomerangs. Sometimes we would walk along the foreshore. Above Yarra Bay, the next cove along, was an impressive large house; my mum said it was Yarra Bay House, a home for orphaned Aboriginal children. I was saddened for those kids—I couldn't think how awful it would be to lose one's parents. But when I said I wanted to offer them comfort, my mother told me we couldn't visit them.

When Tim told me of his grandsons, Jack and Steve, and their Aboriginal heritage, all my sensibilities were alerted—especially as 'Weabonga' is an Aboriginal word, and I presumed this meant the place had an extensive Aboriginal history. I hoped the two boys could be proud of their patrimony and comfortable with their identities. If I could assist them as their teacher, I was determined to do so.

After that chat with Tim I spent even more time with Jack, ensuring he felt included in everything, and that he had many chances to talk about himself and his ideas and wishes. My own wish was for him to have the best possible opportunities that schooling could offer. In my interactions with him, I wasn't trying to be a counsellor, psychologist or social worker, as that wasn't my role; I did what I thought was appropriate, as a teacher, to facilitate his development and happiness. I figured that success in schoolwork would help him open up to other experiences and possibilities in life.

All four of the Grade Fives were amenable and willing in their interactions with me and with their school tasks. They quickly learnt that they were free to make decisions about several matters, such as the order in which to do a morning's activities, and their selection of materials for craft work, subjects for written narratives, books to read for pleasure and so on. As we progressed through the first year together, I came to leave a growing number of decisions open to them; never once did they betray my confidence.

In Grade Five there are challenging skills to learn in language and maths. Imagine trying to bring long division of pounds, shillings and pence under control; just try to solve a long division of 320 pounds, five shillings and five pence by thirty-five. Imagine having to form perfect paragraphs, each with a topic sentence, in a story or description.

Our Grade Five group always did their best. I could challenge them to include in their stories a sentence commencing with a past or present participle and another beginning with an adverbial phrase, and all could do so. I could ask them to construct a circle with a radius of three inches, showing segmentation with four right-angled triangles, and all could do so. And I could ask that they conduct the Grade Twos in a flashcard-reading exercise; they could all do so, and enjoyed the opportunity to be in charge and of assistance. They took to their role as the senior students with pride and responsibility.

17

I found myself always welcome with Paul, George, Barbara and Elizabeth. In those winter days it was especially warming to be made to feel an integral part of their family. How generous they were, opening up their home and including me in everything. Being with these good folk was settling, allowing me to concentrate on my responsibilities. It gave me a chance, finally, to enjoy my appointment as teacher-in-charge. I could feel myself growing in professional confidence and in a willingness to be fully available to the children each day.

The wife and mother of the family was never discussed nor was her absence explained to me. I gathered she had died. There were no images of her displayed anywhere in the rooms of the home to which I had access, and I saw no family album occasionally looked at in reverie. I respected the family's silence and had no intention of disturbing it, but I was intrigued and also a little concerned that they never spoke of so grievous a loss. Judging from the family's kindness and hospitality to me,

I thought the mother must have been an exceptional woman. Paul, and his sisters Barbara and Elizabeth were very considerate, down-to-earth and genuine, so I believed the mother to have been a positive role model who had great sway over them all. Silently I thanked her for her influence and for helping me—through her children—in difficult times.

Being so grateful to the family, I cooperated and assisted in every way open to me. On workdays Paul was always outdoors somewhere on the property, trying to achieve as much as possible in the daylight. George, elderly and many years retired, milked the house cow every morning, and then spent his days resting on the veranda or, in winter, in front of the fire, reading any newspaper that reached the home or listening to the ABC local radio. Whenever Barbara or Elizabeth was at home, the dutiful daughter kept house and garden in fine order, made jams and preserves from fruits in season, baked cakes and biscuits, washed and ironed, and cooked the evening meal.

Although I was never asked to lend a hand in the farm chores, as I was far too busy with my work for that, I soon discovered there were many tasks I could take on after arriving home in the late afternoon.

It became a routine that I managed the lighting. Up to four pressure lanterns were lit at night, and all required regular cleaning, replacement of gauze wicks, filling with fuel and, finally, lighting. Achieving a bright, steady and even light wasn't always easy, and I prided myself on the speed and competence I developed as a lamplighter. By the time Paul came in from the paddocks each evening, indoors was bright and welcoming.

The chooks were free range all day, laying eggs wherever the fancy struck them. The eggs then had to be collected each night, otherwise the goannas or snakes would make a meal of them. Chooks had many favoured laying spots, all sheltered, such as under the shearing shed or within a hedge; to lay an egg a chook needs a sense of security, so they prefer to be hidden from birds of prey, reptiles and other predators. Finding the eggs became a treasure hunt that I mostly enjoyed as I got to wander around the paddock on my own in the evening light. It was relaxing—that is, unless I had to crawl under the shed with all the sheep droppings, or in reaching for an egg I also found a lurking snake. I didn't mind the red-bellied blacks, but the browns worried me, as they could be aggressive and vicious. If I stamped my foot the blacks would slither away, but I never stamped at a brown. I would back away slowly and cautiously—the serpent could have the prize. There were so many chooks that the homestead always enjoyed a full store of fresh eggs with rich yellow yolks.

When shearing time came, an extra pair of hands was very welcome. My sister had married a grazier and, in my early teens, I had spent several school holidays on their Western Plains property. I'd taken up opportunities there to practise as a shed rouseabout and to learn to press a bale of wool; as a city lad, I'd really enjoyed the experience. I'd noticed Paul's increasing anxiety as the shearing week approached. 'What's the weather forecast?' he'd asked. 'Have you spoken with Bill or Monica in the last few days? Did you hear whether Bill's recovered from his bout of flu and ready for our shearing?' So, I volunteered to return home as soon as school finished each day of shearing week and help out in the shed for a few hours. On those afternoons I would pick and skirt fleeces, prepare and load the wool press, and press bales.

Wool presses then were entirely manual. As the kids had learnt, the considerable force needed to compress a pile of fleeces into a packed bale was produced through a long handle on the press, acting as a lever. This made wool pressing skilful work. Any bales I produced—although not packed quite as tight or weighing in as heavily as an experienced presser might have achieved—always topped the mark of three hundred pounds. Each was then judged fit enough for me to apply the station stencil.

Max and Bill from the village were both working in the shed. I'd met them at the Sunday tennis games, and had the occasional chat but now had a chance to get to know them better in different circumstances. They were happy souls, chiacking and joshing me, but I could do the work, enjoyed it, and accepted their banter in good grace. We would all share a coldie at the end of the day.

Each evening I always washed and wiped the dishes over the sink, chatting away with whichever daughter was presently at home. Through such interactions, they decided I could take care of basic cooking if necessary.

As both women were nursing sisters, they were a boon to the area. Locals called on them from time to time to tend wounds, determine the cause of fevers, advise on severity of symptoms and, generally, act as community nurses. Their mother, I learnt from Tim at the PO, had first come to Weabonga as the official bush nurse, so the girls were carrying on in her footsteps.

Sometimes the dutiful daughter would be called away for many hours, even overnight, and I would prepare the evening meal for the three men left at home. In no way was I a replacement for the daughters, as both were excellent cooks, but I could get an edible meal on the table. It was clear that neither Elizabeth nor Barbara resented giving up their professional, nursing lives to spend their time at home with their father, but it was also easy to see they would have preferred to be working away at a regional or base hospital; without design, the time each daughter spent away from the home tending to locals became longer, and my role as cook became more routinely relied on. Eventually I was asked if I would take on the role on a more permanent basis. As I liked the family so much, I was prepared to give it a try. Being away from what I really wanted—the city, friends, family, further study and Patricia—I understood what the daughters were experiencing. I said I was willing to become the fallback cook as long as all understood my need to spend time each night preparing for school. I couldn't become a housekeeper or a vegetable gardener, although I'd help where I could. We reached agreement happily, and from that point neither daughter stayed for any lengthy period at the farm.

Relying on some fine, old, rudimentary country cookbooks, I tried to vary my methods and the ingredients each night, so our palates didn't become too jaded. Lamb and mutton were the main meats I dealt with, and an occasional fowl, rabbit or hare. My sense of taste for lamb became acute, and I could tell Paul from which paddock he had chosen the animal; sheep meat always reflects exactly what the animal has been grazing, and some paddocks had more subterranean clover, introduced and spread by Paul to enhance the quality of the pasture, or rye grass than others.

Neither Paul nor George ever criticised the meals I presented, but I guess neither thought it wise to complain, either.

⌒

The farmhouse was a solid weatherboard with three bedrooms. As George was in one and one of the daughters in another, Paul had to share with me. He wasn't used to this; being the only boy, he'd always enjoyed a room to himself. On the other hand, growing up I had always shared with my brother, just eighteen months older than I, and we'd learnt to get along and to cooperate. I asked Paul whether he could accept the change and was reassured by his positive response. Fortunately neither of us was a noisy sleeper, and because Paul worked strenuously he went off to sleep easily and quickly. I was most grateful that he was prepared to give up his privacy so I could have a home.

As soon as the spring weather arrived, Paul announced he was moving his bed to the veranda. He explained he did this each year and spent months sleeping in the fresh air, and that he loved to do so. He invited me to move my bed as well. The veranda was long and wide, offering plenty of room for both of us. We slept on the east-facing side, with Virginia creeper providing some shade all along its length. From our beds, through gaps in the creeper, we could watch the moon and stars in their travels across the sky. Night noises entertained us: those of birds, crickets, foxes and frogs. A powerful owl roosted sometimes in a gum in the house paddock, just a little distance from where we lay; we never heard him but enjoyed watching his swift, silent gliding to and from his perch. The rising sun, rays broken only by the creeper, would wake us. It was delicious to sleep so soundly with little between us and the great world but a few bedclothes.

It didn't go unnoticed by me that although I'd been desperately unhappy sleeping on the O'Callaghan veranda behind my tar-paper wall, I was now blissfully sleeping on the Williamson veranda. Open-air sleeping was a source of delight when all other of life's necessary elements were in place.

Life was pleasant with the Williamsons. In winter, after the evening meal and the cleaning up, shared by us all, we sat in the lounge with a fire always glowing and two pressure lights allowing us to read or for me to work on school materials. We might have the radio playing in the background, always on the ABC, or perhaps a battery-powered LP record-player. We also chatted a lot. George was always pretty up to date with news, and that year he was engrossed in the US presidential race as John F. Kennedy faced Nixon in a series of debates. Paul, a sports fanatic, would always want to talk about the latest cricket or rugby scores.

In November we all welcomed JFK as the first Catholic President of the United States. As a 'rock chopper' myself at the time, I was pleased by his win, but we all had a sense of excitement about the possibilities he would open up for the United States and for the world. He was a significant person for the planet, we all agreed.

I also had a personal interest in JFK. He'd been baptised with Fitzgerald as his middle name; his mother, Rose, had been a Fitzgerald, and his maternal grandfather—John Francis 'Honey Fitz' Fitzgerald—had been a congressman and the Mayor of Boston. My own paternal grandmother had been a Fitzgerald before marriage, and my oldest sister had traced JFK's family back to his Irish Fitzgerald roots, finding a direct link to our ancestors: JFK and I shared a great-great-grandfather. We were third cousins, or so my sister claimed. I felt huge pride in this connection, tenuous though I saw it to be. When JFK's ancestors and my own had arrived in their lands of choice, far from their homeland, they'd all had very little. Through dint of hard work, both branches of the family, each in a new nation separated by the Pacific, had become established and progressed well.

Having no personal ambition to be Australia's prime minister—although from an early age, my mother had included that possibility in her dreams for me—I had no plan to emulate JFK. It strengthened me, though, to know what was possible. I doubled down on my resolve that my time in Weabonga would be put to good purpose as one important stage in a longer trip. My journey, I thought, might eventually lead to a headship of a large public school, but perhaps—I dreamt with JFK's crisp, clipped, clear Boston-accented voice murmuring softly in my ear—there would be other destinations as well. Whatever was to be, I determined to make each stage rewarding in some manner.

A few weeks after JFK's election we listened, late one afternoon in December, to the exciting conclusion of the Australia versus West Indies cricket test being played in Brisbane. It ended in a tie, one of only two in test cricket history.

George spoke much about the upheavals in Africa: not only of the massacres and riots in South Africa, but the fact that colony after colony on that continent was achieving independence. Africa was really stirring, and there was pushback from the colonisers. In late March, a couple of months before I'd moved in with the Williamsons, news had come of the disgraceful Sharpeville massacre in South Africa. I'd been greatly disturbed when I'd heard that white police officers had murdered sixty-nine black Africans and injured 180 others. Out of these, they had killed ten children and injured nineteen others. When it was reported that the children had been present at the demonstration not to challenge the pass laws, which restricted movement for blacks, but to advocate for a chance to receive a secondary education, I couldn't help but think of our Weabonga youngsters. How precious they were to us all, and how we all knew we must support their chances to live with dignity and meaning.

The world was changing around us, while our days and evenings were mostly unchanging in Weabonga. There was no sense of a rut developing, just a healthy, calm playing out of what had become routine.

Tim, the retired postmaster, eventually told me what had happened to George's wife. 'Following on World War II, everything remained in limited supply around here,' he recounted. 'No one had petrol to run machinery. For a number of years after the war, everyone relied on horses, either in the saddle or driving a sulky or dray.

'One Saturday afternoon in 1946, the Williamsons attended a sports day at the local sports ground. You know that? It's on the common, just up around the next bend on the Limbri Road. On completion of the sports and just at dusk, George settled his wife and young Paul in their sulky. Paul was about eleven years of age, I think. They set off towards their homestead—not a great distance, as you know.'

'As they bowled along, the inside wheel of the sulky mounted a large rock. It must have tumbled onto the road following the families passing to the sports earlier in the day. Apparently in the growing dark, George, holding the reins, hadn't seen the damn thing.'

I was apprehensive about where this story was going, but listened avidly.

'The sulky gave a great lurch. It almost tipped over before coming back to rest on both wheels. The jolt was so violent it threw Mrs Williamson right out of the vehicle. She fell heavily and must have hit her head on a rock beside the road. By the time George had the sulky halted and rushed back to her, she was dead.'

Tim paused, then continued. 'Her death affected everybody in the district. She was a well-loved woman. Everyone had felt her kindness or generosity in some way, so we were all deeply distressed by her loss.'

Tim stopped again, and I sat quietly waiting for him to tell me more.

'The effect on George was immediate. The instant she died, he changed. He'd been friendly and outgoing, but became quiet and reserved. He just avoided contact outside his family. He drew in on himself and his children. The four daughters, all still teenagers or in their early twenties, had to take over the house. They took on everything their mother had done. They were wonderful. It was those four who finished raising Paul.'

George had still cared for his family, ensuring that all the children had opportunities for education, and that the girls had as many choices as possible.

'Although,' Tim said, 'from the moment of his wife's death, George wasn't as easy with his children as they may have liked. He seemed distant somehow, and he was angrier. I think the kids not only lost their mum, but they might have lost their dad in some ways as well that day.'

My own experience of George was that he was a good, kind man who'd invited me into his home when I really needed support. I admired him and what he had achieved for his children. It was clear they all loved him, even if warily, and I felt great warmth for him as well. By the time I joined the family, he had handed most responsibilities for the property to Paul. I was aware of some tensions in their relationship, but Paul's succession was well in progress. The son frequently asked for his father's advice, which was given following serious thought. There was never any sense that George wasn't involved in important decisions, so whatever Paul's final choices, George generally accepted them.

Often on Saturday mornings, as I drove with father and son to Tamworth for the afternoon rugby game, the two discussed important matters such as the timing of the shearing, the team they should contract in for that wool clip, the amount of superphosphate to be spread on the top paddock, or the stud from which to purchase new rams. I enjoyed listening in, as I learnt a lot about farming and property management. And I occasionally put forth my ideas. I remember saying, on one of these drives, 'When I visited my sister on their sheep station, Honeybugle outside Nyngan, my brother-in-law purchased his rams from some well-known studs around Warren. I've forgotten their names, but the rams were huge, impressive brutes, with thick fleece.'

'Oh! That might have been Haddon Rig. Their rams are sure huge, and their wool is great, but they don't suit us.'

Eager to learn—and unaware of the possibility I was being a bit tiresome—I asked, 'In what way not suited? They looked terrific to me.'

'Well,' George replied, with some patience, 'they're big, long-bodied brutes. They're bred to travel great distances across flat plains country, moving from water to water. Dams there can be a fair way apart. Here, we need sheep that can handle our hills. Water here is all around, so our sheep don't walk far at any time. We need smaller, sturdier animals, and we need sheep that can cope with snow and frost. We buy our rams from the studs around Armidale and Walcha. Their local rams suit our conditions and our flocks better.'

Grateful for the lesson and the patience, I would withdraw from the conversation and let the two sheep men talk any problem through. By the time we reached Tamworth, solutions would have been identified. There was little acrimony and, mostly, mutually agreed outcomes.

I was able to find a level of contentment with this family— enough to get me through my obligatory two years, at least.

18

The children loved music and singing, and most could carry a tune. By the second half of that first year we had developed a repertoire.

Each evening, Tom and Debbie would sit with their large family on the veranda at home in the dusk or starlight, all singing along together. They enjoyed creating harmonies and tonal effects.

The Teegan family, with Lindie and Susie, spent most Sundays attending church, where their lay preacher dad, Vic, would conduct the singing. These two girls knew lots of songs and were happy to sing them for their classmates.

But all the children had favourite songs and suggested tunes for our school to learn. Many were of the country-and-western genre and didn't particularly appeal to me, but I was happy for the kids to be singing with enjoyment—if the songs were about faithful old dogs and unrideable horses, then so be it.

I loved music. Tunes ran along in my head as an accompaniment to my thoughts. But I couldn't play an instrument, not even the wooden recorder to which I'd been introduced at teachers' college. I could carry a tune in the right key, though, and I had a trusty tuning fork to give us all a middle C starter. I could read enough music to nut out the starting note of a song and, generally, work out the tune. And the wonderful ABC School Broadcasts ran several music programs, including choral singing, each week. So, I thought, our tiny school could have a music curriculum of reasonable sorts.

Early on I decided the school needed both a radio and a record-player. The former was easy to obtain: I'd brought back a battery radio from that first Easter break in Sydney. But the record-player had to wait until a request to the parents was answered. The Parents and Citizens Group arranged a little raffle, and with the funds raised we purchased a good-quality, battery-operated LP player.

Each morning the two Grade Ones listened to the 'Kindergarten of the Air' broadcast, hearing much that I couldn't bring them otherwise, and they both found it great fun. Once a week the ABC introduced new songs to learn. The radio presenters would break a song into phrases, send a model performance of each phrase from the studio musicians, and then encourage the remote children to repeat these with the help of their teacher. Gradually each song would be built up phrase by phrase, and by the broadcast's end the kids could generally perform it. Not all these songs became favourites, but they were easily remembered and would be sung with the minimum of encouragement.

A child would sometimes request that a favourite song be taught to the whole group and, if all agreed, we would add such tunes to the repertoire. By July the younger and older children each had a set they preferred. But they all sang, with delight, about fifteen songs in common.

With limited music in most of their homes, school was the children's main chance to hear something different and to extend their insights into the many forms that music might take. The ABC Schools Broadcast also had a weekly program encouraging upper-primary children to appreciate many kinds of music; the older kids listened avidly to these sessions and followed up by discussing what had struck them about the pieces presented. Once we had our record-player I built a small collection of material, with LPs often suggested by the children to which they would return time after time. Music was a vital component of the school curriculum, as I didn't want these isolated children to miss out.

⌣

The record-player enabled us to try an exciting activity: dancing! By clearing the desks to the edges of the room, we could create ample space. Winter had brought on some bleak days, and dancing warmed body and spirit. And my observation of the kids swinging in time and tapping their feet when they were singing strengthened my impression that moving to music is a natural behaviour for children.

The kids embraced folk dancing wholeheartedly and with much enthusiasm. We commenced with simple dances such as 'The Grand Old Duke of York', which the youngest could easily follow. We did 'Strip the Willow' together; all could dance the required steps and remember the easy progressions. The older children began to want more intricate routines and steps but remained open to dancing frequently with the young ones.

We all danced at least once a week, and even more if the lesson schedule for basic skills permitted. Dancing was never held up as a reward for the completion of set tasks in English or maths, but the children soon worked out that it might follow if all completed their written work. Standards weren't allowed to drop, but dancing began to figure more often as the kids were motivated and keen.

They also loved to perform plays. Activities to extend the English syllabus included drama production, and each *School Magazine* carried a short play written especially for children. We would enjoy choosing a play, auditioning for parts and selecting performers while ensuring that all the students had a frequent and fair chance to participate. Then we'd practise and perform the play for the entertainment of the other students.

Drawing on the children's singing, dancing and drama perform-ances, we often entertained ourselves with impromptu concerts. The kids had more than enough content for a full program.

The children's love of dancing brought back memories of bright times when Patricia and I had danced and felt close. Together we had often accepted invitations to balls.

The routine associated with these events was very enjoyable to both of us. Patricia would dress up in a gown, while I'd wear a tuxedo or dress suit, and I'd give her a corsage that matched her dress.

We would attend a decorated ballroom, usually in special locations such as the Hotel Australia in Martin Place. We'd revel in the semi-formality of the evening and enjoy the supper provided with proper waiter service. Then we'd dance through the night to a classy orchestra while mixing with a happy crowd. The night usually ended around 1 a.m.

We especially enjoyed the Clan Mcleod events, with their mix of modern dance music and traditional Scottish melodies and tunes, where we joined in Highland eightsome reels and Scottish country dancing mixed in with the usual ballroom fare of foxtrots, quicksteps and jazz waltzes.

Just occasionally, if encouraged, an orchestra might break into a very staid, timorous rendition of a standard rock number. We would still manage to jitterbug—quite a feat, given Patricia's voluminous gowns. I loved to rock, and she joined in to ensure my happiness. Being active together brought happiness to both of us.

One thing about me that had first attracted Patricia's attention had been my singing voice. When my mates and I had parties, each performed a special song that had become identified with the individual. A party night wasn't complete until we had, once again, heard the entire repertoire. Pat, who'd been a choirboy at St Mary's Cathedral until his voice broke, sang at every party, no matter the time of year, the carol 'Silent Night'. His twist was to sing it in German. From Don we heard 'Too Young', a Nat King Cole number, but Don lacked Nat's smoothness—we didn't mind. Leo gave us a rocking version of 'Tutti Frutti'. Peter and Ronny varied their numbers but always came good. All joined in each song after the first verse or so, and everyone sang the choruses. A barbershop quartet we never were, and, as Kenso boys, we never got close to the Four Seasons.

My own speciality was the songs of Johnny O'Keefe, Australia's first real rock icon—and Patricia liked these songs. A slim basis for a long-term relationship, perhaps, but it was serving us well. Every Saturday morning call included a rendition of at least one song; generally, because of the geographical separation, it was 'Over the Mountain'. That song allowed me to display the full range of my abilities, and I belted it out into the phone with gusto and bravura. Perhaps if I'd known then what was later revealed, that my friend invited both her Melbourne flatmates to listen in when my singing commenced, I might have been less forthright and expressive.

19

Each winter Saturday, Paul and I played with the Tamworth team, allowing me to make real friendships among the rugby crowd.

While I was a bit of a blow-in to the scene, most were locals happily engaged in a life they would continue to lead, without much change, into the future. Many of my fellow players were from a farm property and set to inherit the land; others were building up a practice or business, or improving an established family concern in town. Their horizons didn't need to move much beyond the district. They were finding marriage partners, establishing links to support them over their lives, building supportive neighbourhoods and communities, and investing in a future that would be best for the families they planned to nurture. It seemed they'd decided that mixing with the rugby crowd would help them to achieve their goals, and this was clear-sighted; within the rugby scene were solid money and significant social influence.

I, on the other hand, was investing in a happy experience for the short term. My own search for a marriage partner appeared to be well in hand, and the city setting in which I might choose to make a more permanent home was getting clearer in my mind. After seven months in Weabonga I'd decided my future needed intellectual stimulation, opportunities for further study, a continuing life for the mind, access to music and theatre, and a solid group of like-minded friends to help bring these dreams to fruition. I had committed to the two years of obligatory country service, and now I was certain that rural living couldn't supply what I needed to be happy and fulfilled. That wasn't to dismiss country life, which I viewed as a great choice for many, especially for raising children—it just wasn't for me.

Most of my Tamworth rugby pals were then unmarried and without serious attachments. They were particularly keen to meet young ladies, and there were many attractive and fine women who found the lads of the club congenial company.

From the games and the socialising, a group of friends emerged, young men and women whom I joined most weekends for leisure time. If there was no rugby game scheduled, each Saturday we all met up in the upstairs lounge bar of the Tudor Hotel, just before lunch. There we planned the remainder of the weekend: the races at Somersby, a picnic, a visit to a friend's property, a concert, a play, some musical theatre at the Tamworth Amateur Theatrical Society. Still being reliant on Paul for transport to and from Weabonga, I couldn't often stay overnight in Tamworth. Infrequently an alternative lift was available, so I spent some Saturday nights sleeping in the home of a friend in town, saving me the trip back to Weabonga until late on the Sunday afternoon.

During the rugby season, our teams travelled each Saturday morning to the distant towns where we were to play. Such trips were always full of camaraderie, and the competition in which Tamworth played produced a high standard of football. A past captain of the Australian Wallabies, Peter Fenwicke, played for the Walcha team, and we always had spirited and tough games against them. Our country district's team was strong and skilled enough to almost beat the visiting British Lions in a game played in front of several thousand people on the Tamworth oval. Games against Quirindi—where the team was made up of matey but competitive men, with supporters who were the friendliest of all the towns we visited—were those I enjoyed most.

But the most memorable Saturday was spent in Walcha, playing in a snowstorm. Our club couldn't field two full teams that day, as many players had come down with winter illnesses or been injured. When volunteers were called for to make up numbers, I put my hand up to play in both scheduled matches. Although I was a forward, I was asked to fill in on the wing for the second game. On a slushy, muddy field sprinkled with snow, this game developed into a forwards' slugfest, as games in such conditions often do. Backs simply can't make rapid runs in mud and couldn't, at least that day, make rapid passing rushes with frozen hands. Clouds of steam rose above every ruck and maul.

Being stuck near the sideline as winger, with nothing much to do, I have never, ever been so cold. My breath came out in thick white clouds. My limbs shook. I took to making runs up and down the line, or jumping on the spot, always keeping an eye on the game, and when possible rushing in to the forward fray, rucking and mauling away—anything to keep warm. O, Walcha! O cold the black-frost Walcha day.

As a forward, although easily the lightest of any of the 'pigs', I varied between taking the field as hooker, front row or breakaway. I didn't much care where, as long as I played. My footy skills were never going to see me advance far, so I didn't build any ambition to be a specialist prop or deadly breakaway. But I enjoyed playing, and the rugby scene was a great one for a young, unmarried fellow.

Or, at least, it should have been. But occasional bubbles of discontent surfaced among the club members, and I had concerns for Paul.

～

Though I could sometimes spend nights away from Weabonga, enjoying concerts or balls or parties, Paul wasn't so carefree. He was devoted to the farm, determined to run it successfully and doing a great job. In the time I lived with him, he added to the fertility of the pastures through programs of subterranean clover and super spreading, and built up the numbers and quality of his flocks. He spent every night at his homestead.

Paul didn't dance, either, so didn't accept invitations to balls. His only chance to meet young women was at the rugby club. He was much admired there as a fine and courageous player; it was widely believed he would eventually play for his country if only he could be noticed by the national selectors. He'd already been chosen in the regional teams, which played against visiting national teams or took part in intrastate carnivals. He was good company, and his fellow players enjoyed being with him. But while he would have enjoyed having a girlfriend, circumstances were against him.

George wasn't in great health—the poor man's rattling cough was terrible and distressing to hear. The dutiful daughters made it clear that once their father didn't need their care, their lives would be played out somewhere other than the Weabonga farm. So my friend would be left alone on the property. He didn't want that, and I didn't want that for him.

I told him about all the available young women I met at balls, many of them attractive, pleasant, intelligent and competent. And my friend was just the sort for whom these country girls were looking: a pastoralist running a property of two thousand acres that he would inherit in time. I was happy to play Cupid—but I couldn't get him to cooperate.

Although we became quite good friends, we were typical young men of the time, rarely speaking about emotional matters and not sharing our closest thoughts. So, Paul and I never spoke about his reluctance to seek out a steady girlfriend.

My mother used to repeat to me an Irish saying: 'You can't have two women on the same floor.' I took this to mean that in Ireland a young man shouldn't marry and bring his wife to live in his family home if his mother was still alive. That way lay trouble, so young Irish men were loath to marry if they couldn't strike out on their own, instead leaving the family hearth to their mother's control. This helped explain why there were so many middle-aged Irish bachelors, or so it was claimed.

My friend obviously wasn't in such a position, but I wondered if he'd decided that while his father was alive and his sisters were still often staying at home, he couldn't or shouldn't bring a girlfriend into their lives. Or perhaps he was afraid to replace his mother totally as the woman of the house, which would mean that she was really gone forever. How sad for my friend to lose her when he was a young lad. I could understand his holding on to her in memory, if that was the case.

In our Saturday phone conversations, Patricia expressed pleasure in my new-found friendships and happier way of life, and I reported my own gladness that she'd settled down well in Melbourne.

One morning she told me of 'falling on her feet' in a new job she'd recently accepted. After starting as an assistant to the news director of Melbourne's Channel 7, she had moved quickly to the more important role of assistant to the station's general manager. In that position she was the senior female employee at the company and enjoyed the challenges of getting live television to air.

Surrounded by creative people, she formed friends with a tight group whom she nicknamed her 'rat pack'. She was mixing with directors, producers, talent and announcers, and she described them as a witty, convivial, intelligent set that made her work life special, and her social life interesting and rewarding.

Our chats were rich as we both had much news to share, and we each enjoyed the world of the other. Our milieus were vastly different: big-city sophistication and leading-edge technology contrasted with down-to-earth country style and a party line phone that had a crank handle. We marvelled that Australia contained such contrasts, and that we two were embedded in such totally different lives.

But each of our conversations brought us closer together, for we continued to share so much: young people finding their way to their own place in the world, while coming to better understand themselves and each other.

20

My younger pupils remained relatively unformed. When I interacted with the older students, I could glimpse the adult solidifying from their developing components. But for the youngsters, possibilities remained open—almost nothing had jelled.

The first impression the younger boys gave was the mass of their group, its physicality. Between Grades One and Four there were eleven of them, ranging from six to ten years of age. The first cousins—Will, Rick, Robbie and Gary—dominated the group without eclipsing the others.

The youngest, Charlie, was easily distinguished. Though I'd shared a home with him for the first several weeks in the village, I had come to know him only a little—very little—on his own while I was there. He was chubby and timid. He had a slight speech problem, but he didn't speak much and initiated communication rarely. I worried about him more than any other pupil, so I devoted lots of time to him. My encouragement was working well for him, and he was always a trier, making serious and intense efforts. I would have appreciated an opportunity to discuss ways of supporting such a pupil with an experienced and expert mentor. Charlie made progress, but it wasn't rapid until the days following his inaugural story of helping his dad dump old metal scraps.

Charlie loved painting, drawing and colouring in, and he enjoyed puzzles. When we had folk dancing, singing or physical activities, he came alive and could be somewhat vivacious. He sang along with the group, and when he learnt a tune he would remember it well, much better than words from a text. And when Charlie smiled—slowly, shyly and reservedly—it was a terrific reward.

I sometimes had trouble telling apart the first cousins in Grades Three and Four. They were all the same height, all the same shape, all with similar facial features. There was no sense of differences in maturity among them: they were a unit. They loved being together and were rarely separated, although they easily admitted other boys into their circle. In the schoolroom, they always sat near each other; in the schoolyard, they were always side by side, often with arms slung over shoulders. Away from school they were always together, playing games, rabbiting, collecting firewood and rambling through the bush.

Over my two years with them, I saw them grow increasingly into replicas of their dads. This was just what they seemed to want, and their dads were great models for them. I imagined these nuggety little guys growing up into a formidable team of shearers, strong and powerful, just below average height—and, through their solidarity, a bit intimidating to any grazier who questioned their tallies or shearing style.

Academically, these boys travelled along reasonably well. They built up their sight-word libraries and wrote acceptable stories with a variety of sentence types. They began to try writing with some order while using paragraphs. They remembered more and more maths facts and could almost automatically apply their times tables. Anything to do with numbers in agriculture caught their attention and application.

Joe and Jimmy, the boys whose mother, Marie, had failed to shoot a roo, were in Grades Four and Two. Both did well academically, not just keeping up but getting ahead. Engaging cheerfully in all school activities, they were always a reliable source of humour and attempted witticisms.

Joe, who had begun the raucous laughter at his mum's poor aim, looked for fun in most things. He encouraged his fellow pupils to join in, and they did in their own reserved ways, genuine in the smiles and quiet chuckles he elicited from them. Joe could be a lot of fun—I just sometimes had to guide him towards acceptable targets for his humour.

It was Joe who referred to the inspector Mr Flood as 'more a trickle than a flood', following his visit in the third term.

'Good one,' I acknowledged, as the gibe had caught the reticence and gentleness that Mr Flood had adopted with the children.

On his visits, the inspector always appeared in a pinstriped blue suit, looking more like a bank manager than a schoolteacher, so the children found him distant and, I suppose, aloof. He didn't mean to be: he was always pleasant and easy with me, and aimed to be so with the children.

It was also Joe who asked, 'How did you get on with the inspector?'

I'd told the kids that the inspector's visit was about my performance rather than theirs, and they weren't to be concerned if Mr Flood asked any of them questions or looked over their work. Joe seemed pleased when I answered honestly that my inspection had gone well and I'd been found worthy of appointment as a permanent teacher, no longer on probation.

I had no doubt that Mr Flood's visit had been much discussed over the Wallace family dinner table—I felt sure Joe hadn't found the ideas he expressed on his own.

Jimmy was a true delight: always smiling, always happy, often charming. Sailing through his work, he talked to me freely about everything that interested him and asked many questions, with a well-developed curiosity in the world around him. I often thought a class full of children just like Jimmy would be a teacher's heaven.

⌣

There were six more of the younger group. Mike, Phil, Charlie's brothers and the other O'Callaghan lads from my first village home were very reserved and hesitant in entering into any discussion. Lots of encouragement would produce a response, but they rarely volunteered an answer or made suggestions to their peers. When I instructed or coached them directly, they responded appropriately, attending well, so their learning was fine, and gradually both were gaining knowledge and skills in the curriculum areas. These two older boys of Lawrie and Jill were thin and spare. *Like little whips*, I thought. A bit awkward and skittish, they had to be treated with care and sensitivity.

In the other Grade Four lad, Mark, there was a looseness of limb. He walked with a loping, easy action, and he had fluidity in all his movements. This didn't always give him superiority in the kicking ball and running games in which the boys readily engaged. There was an element of grace in Mark's actions, accompanied by quickness in his intellect. He was curious about the world, loved life and never seemed daunted by any challenge. He enjoyed sharing his interests with the others but was also quite happy to pursue his own interests, savouring academic work.

Mark kept pace with our goals and set himself additional ones when time permitted. He asked many, many questions but was not demanding, although he couldn't be overlooked. He could be quite content on his own and wasn't a leader with his peers, never wanting to cause them to rally to his ideas, and I noticed they found his frequent questioning curious. Of all the children, I believed he would have flourished most in a school with library facilities, art rooms and choices of subjects. There was always a half smile and a quiet amusement about him—at only nine, perhaps he was already developing a sense of irony. Sometimes when he assayed a little sally to another child, Mark would look at me and we'd nod to each other: we both got it, even if no one else had.

We shared a nod and a smile one day after he made a suggestion to Lindie. Every child knew that she enjoyed trying out any new activity; she didn't push herself forward to be first, but we all recognised her happiness when allowed to be so.

As we were about to tackle a new skill in craft work, Mark said, 'Lindie, would you like to go first?'

He looked at me. We gave each other a subdued, easy nod of acknowledgement.

His remark illustrated to me the support the children gave each other. He wasn't inferring a criticism of Lindie or meaning any harm—he was actually delighted that she could get so much enjoyment from such a simple thing, but he also saw the funny side.

The youngest girl, Susie, was very similar to the charming boy, Steve, one of her Grade Two classmates: they were likeable, quick and friendly little people. Susie had some of her older sister's sense of fun but unlike Lindie was never overly excited. Academically, Susie seemed to me the most gifted of all the children. She read well, she easily gained proficiency in beginner maths, she wrote interesting little stories with some complexity, and she chose to spend lots of any free time in reading for pleasure.

The sessions I had with the three Grade Twos, Steve, Susie and Carol, were always enjoyable. They soaked up my attention, and Susie and Steve were such quick learners that they picked up any point of instruction with ease. Carol, a small, neat child, needed more of my attention; she was a quiet girl, a little overshadowed by her two shining classmates, so I made certain to be attentive to her whenever I could.

Steve and Susie would giggle while pretending to chide each other. Susie would say, if she was a little slower in completing a learning task than Steve, 'Oh, I'm such a slowcoach, just a silly thing.'

Not to be outdone, Steve would return, 'No. I'm the dumbcluck.'

If I overheard these exchanges, I'd chime in. 'Good-oh. What will we do with the two of you?'

How charming they were, and I took enjoyment from their obvious confidence. That they could denigrate their own performances suggested to me they were keenly aware they were competent learners, and that pleased me enormously.

21

There were unexpected bonuses of moving in with the Williamsons. One was being introduced to a set of people I'd never before met: the other local landholders. They didn't use the village and hadn't need of the school. With their own phones in their homesteads and Bon's mail car stopping by their gates each week, they never needed to visit the Weabonga PO. So I'd never met them, even though they lived all around me.

Paul explained that the local propertied families had always been hospitable. Now that their fleeces were attracting high value once more, they could celebrate and begin to entertain again. When the Williamsons received invitations to dinner, I was expected to attend with my host family. How enjoyable these outings were.

Between Weabonga and Limbri there were about twenty sheep stations. Along the Limbri Road the properties had frontages of about one and a half miles both to the road and to the creek, and the best land on each farm was that abutting the creek. Nowhere was flat, but in those paddocks the slopes were reasonably gentle, the trees had been cleared years earlier, and the pasture was improved with clover and an agricultural innovation, super spreading.

Earlier, Australian farmers had learned of the swift growth grasses and clovers could experience when their fields were spread with superphosphate as a fertiliser. Much of the superphosphate, or 'super' as it was more generally known, came from the Pacific island of Nauru, where seabirds had roosted and deposited huge piles of guano. Mining and sale of super had assisted Nauru economically and wealth was spreading, in turn, for Australia's farmers as super became more widely used. Paul had been an eager adopter of super enrichment.

This creek-side land carried good numbers of sheep per acre. Away from the creek, the slopes were quite acute. It had been much harder to fell trees in the uplands, so vegetation there could be dense. The slopes were crowned with rocky outcrops and tumbling screes: the realms of tiger snakes and death adders, or so I was told. This land carried less stock, and it was mostly cattle in those back paddocks. At their furthest boundaries, the properties were edged by wilderness. On both sides of the creek, once the cleared lands were crossed, lay huge tracts of government or Crown land. There were no roads into these pristine areas, not even fire trails, but once or twice I rode with others a fair distance into that real bush and camped overnight alongside streams that I felt, probably incorrectly, may have never been seen by white eyes before ours.

Each farming family was isolated and might go for days without meeting someone outside their homestead. Fresh company was very welcome, and invitations between the properties became more frequent. I looked forward especially to visiting two farms.

⌒

About ten miles along the Limbri Road lived a couple who were expert hosts. Allan Watermain was the direct descendant of a famous early Australian explorer and had, in his home, furniture and materials he'd inherited from the earliest days of the colony. The house wasn't more substantial than those of neighbouring homesteads, but the way it was organised and decorated was quite different. In the dining room there was a magnificent cedar table that could seat up to ten; arranged around it was a suite of chairs of matching grace. All stood on a huge Persian carpet, of a size to cover the generous room almost to its edges. The floorboards, which could be seen at the limits of the rug, gleamed with beeswax polish. Against the walls was a pair of sideboards, obviously early colonial, glowing with a burnished deep-red patina. Victorian oils, mostly of scenes of the Arabian desert with Bedouin figures and camels, hung on the walls and suited the atmosphere, bringing a sense of the exotic. There were candles and low lamps creating a subdued air, which drew the focus onto the table and the people sitting around it. This room was the most impressive domestic space that I had yet experienced.

As a host, Allan was witty and laconic, keeping the conversation flowing with ease. His charming wife, Claudine, was as skilful a talker as Allan, so, between them, they created a sense of a country home salon. Claudine was also a wonderful cook, creating special menus from dishes I enjoyed in no other home. A night at their homestead gave me enormous pleasure.

By contrast, their immediate neighbour, Barry White, entertained in his converted dairy: a comfy and snug space made from an unpromising start. There was nothing lavish or exotic when we dined with him—except the host.

I'd met Barry first when motoring with Paul one Sunday in the farm ute; we were foraging for blackberries and mushrooms along the creek. Suddenly we came across a mounted figure. We stopped, as one always did in the country, to say hello and for me to be introduced. I tried to look this stranger right in the eye as we conversed. I didn't want to be seen checking out his attire, but couldn't help doing so.

Barry was naked apart from a G-string affair, a sort of body builder's posing pouch—which, I learnt later, he'd made by cutting down an already skimpy pair of Speedos. This garment barely covered his genitals. He had no pockets, and nowhere to carry his tobacco, papers or matches, which he needed as he was almost a chain smoker. To solve this problem, Barry was wearing a ladies' nylon stocking on his head, with the toe hanging down behind, stuffed with the ingredients for his fags. He chatted with us as though all this was absolutely normal and no cause for comment. I admired his insouciance.

Paul told me of an evening when Barry had come to a dinner at the farm. It was during the 1956 Melbourne Olympic Games, and ABC Radio was rebroadcasting a description of the torch relay's entry into the stadium. A low fire was burning in the grate, and Barry—in a burst of patriotic fervour, perhaps—grabbed up a lighted stick and commenced to run around the lounge with the flame held high. All went well until he ran too near the net curtains, which immediately caught fire. Without so much as a goodbye, Barry continued running, exited the house and wasn't seen again for many weeks.

I never experienced anything quite as exciting as this event when he was present, but we were entertained from time to time by his playing of a harp he'd made from the jawbone of a horse—not quite the biblical jaw of an ass. Barry had trained himself to coax tunes from this instrument, and occasionally I could almost recognise the air he was attempting.

His stories of nature were also memorable. As he worked his property either on horseback or on foot, he explained he could approach animals closely without their noticing. In this way he had witnessed many events and activities involving native animals that few others had seen. I truly enjoyed his tales, as they had, mostly, a ring of truth and revealed quite fascinating aspects of our wildlife. His stories of wedge-tailed eagle behaviour on the ground, for example, were remarkable for his acuity of observation and his ability to bring the birds' actions to life. Ungainly on the earth compared to their aerial grace, the eagle's lumpish hopping and skipping were most comical as he mimicked them—but, as our host made clear, they retained their air of menace. He accurately reproduced the soft caws they made when seemingly conversing, and their harsh cries that warned of any approaching danger. Barry also mimicked the excited whistles of playful eagles as they tumbled and swooped like acrobats in the air.

Occasionally, though, he went a little far. 'Did you know,' he asked one night, 'that deaf adders can enclose their tails with their mouths to form a perfect circle?'

Well, he called them 'deaf adders'. We knew them as death adders. Whatever they were called, they frightened me.

Barry asked, 'Did you know the adder can then bowl itself along, just like a wheel, covering distances with remarkable speed?'

We nodded and smiled.

Occasionally I missed out on such dinners when I was on school holidays or taking a quick weekend break in Sydney.

Twice I flew down to Sydney when Patricia let me know she'd be in the city for a weekend visiting her family. Flying was expensive and quite daunting; older Douglas DC-3 aircraft or more modern but quite small planes were flown in a very bumpy and turbulent way by Butler Air Transport from the Tamworth Airfield, their base. On each of my flights, many people were airsick.

A few times in Sydney I met up with Patricia at Pfahlerts Hotel on Margaret Street, where she might order a Pimm's No. 1 Cup. Pfahlerts was a favourite of ours, as we felt comfortable there together in that elegant setting. We always enjoyed a few happy drinks in the front garden and could chat for hours in amiable contentment.

Pfahlerts was only the start of the evening. We might set off for a movie at the St James or the more upmarket Prince Edward Theatre. Sometimes we took in a foreign film at the

Savoy Cinema, a bijou theatre in Bligh Street, always leaving us with a sense of having experienced European sophistication.

Very occasionally we booked into a show at the Silver Spade Room in the newly opened Chevron Hotel in Kings Cross, Sydney's first four-star accommodation. We had the real pleasure of seeing Ella Fitzgerald one night; we were thrilled by her musicality and ability to improvise, and the ease with which she sang her way into and out of any song. She was generous with her performance, spending some hours on the stage. That nightclub was about as smart and worldly a venue as Sydney could provide and, although attendance almost broke our piggybanks, we enjoyed the sense of being in society. We spent such nights beaming at each other in happiness.

22

The children often coalesced into a single unit, the school cohort. All might be quiet, concentrating on their activities, or more noisy, sharing experiences with a smile on each face. They listened to each other and seldom interrupted, except in eagerness to add a thought, and their conversations would follow a trajectory straightforward and easy for even the youngest to follow. On the first day, the kids had told me that two important things they wanted from school were chances to spend time with each other and to be happy. All through each day, that spirit reigned. They loved being together, and all treated all the others, from oldest to youngest, as their best friends.

Of course, certain preferences were expressed and subgroups formed from time to time. The younger boys certainly liked to play their outdoor games as a little male team; they ran and kicked balls or batted away contentedly without the involvement of the girls. Sometimes, though, Susie would join in with Carol in tow.

'Hey, move aside,' she'd say. 'Let me in, make room for us.'

'Okay. You're on Will's team, and Carol's on Jack's,' was the usual answer.

Vickie, Lindie and Debbie, who enjoyed spending time chatting in a group, might also simply take their place alongside the other players. The game just rolled smoothly on.

When we did our prescribed physical activity sessions, the kids were one group. Tunnel ball, with height-matched teams, was always fun for the whole group: Tom with Charlie on one team, and Jack with Susie on another.

My pupils would request stories, read aloud or invented by me, and sometimes I'd find one that each child could enjoy, in their own way and as appropriate to their age, while listening together. It was remarkable the appeal, for example, an Oscar Wilde fairytale had for all of them: our oldest, Tom, and our youngest, Charlie, would listen enthralled.

Activities executed as a single group reinforced and cemented feelings of unity and solidarity, but such feelings were natural among these children and would have emerged without my deliberate support.

I had heard one-teacher schoolchildren described as forming a 'family'. Among us at Weabonga there were members of eight family groups, but many of the children were kin. We did have older kids sharing the classroom with much younger ones, and this was unusual in a school. So the children were thrust together by circumstance—they chose to come together, though, from their natural instincts. Did this make them a 'family'?

Sometimes people speak of arguments and even feuds as being natural between siblings. Our group never displayed any conflict or disputation, so if negativity is an important component in constituting a family, then our Weabonga group wasn't such.

But the children cared for each other, supported each other and looked after each other as one would hope that family members would do. Tom acted, in the best possible way, as a big brother to all the others. The Grade Five girls would often play a big sister role. There was a solid sense of them being together as one—and if this makes a family, then a family they were.

What did that make me?

At college my lecturers had discussed the 'in loco parentis' relationship that formed the basis for the granting of authority over children: teachers must have authority to perform their role. A literal translation of the term indicates that teachers are 'in place of parents' when a child comes into the school. A teacher must always act in the best interests of all the children and, at all times, keep them safe. Children were forced into the care of schools, so schools had to accept a caring responsibility for them.

I was happy to accept these legal responsibilities, but I wasn't accepting of any broader definition of 'in loco parentis' than the legal interpretation. I wasn't a parent, and I was certainly not the parent of these children. Some aspects of caring for kids were ones that I wouldn't and shouldn't have accepted, but that a parent must. So I didn't think of myself as the father, not even as the 'paterfamilias' or oldest male in the family as ancient Romans had it. I was the teacher, and over those two years I was learning more about that role, gaining skills and working through my doubts.

Like the kids who were made to be at school, in a way I was forced to be teaching at Weabonga. I took it upon myself to continue my professional development, as I received no assistance from my employer, the Department of Education, to do so. I had three visits, each of less than three hours, from Mr Flood in my two years. While I liked the man and he tried to be helpful, there was little he could offer except encouragement, which he gave in huge loads. I was thankful for that, but I was literally on my own. In those two years I met no other teacher and spoke about my work only with the inspector.

Although my professional isolation was complete, I didn't think of myself as anything other than a professional teacher while I was with the children. I wasn't a big brother, I wasn't a paterfamilias, I wasn't a dad. I needed to be proud of my profession, pleased with the choice of occupation I had made as a teenager, and I worked hard to become as good a professional teacher as possible.

There were many challenges—every day, it seemed, gave rise to a pedagogical or broader educational question. I thought deeply, considered what I'd experienced and what I'd learnt at college, analysed my observations, and attempted to derive a solution or answer that would best serve the children. I'd realised early on that my two years at Weabonga would be a great chance to progress as a teacher; I now felt that was happening and that I was learning on the job. But having someone with whom to talk it through would have been so rich and rewarding.

I hoped I was leading the children well, treating them with respect and modelling a professional at work.

⌒

By term three in the first year, I'd never had cause to reprimand a child. Sometimes I redirected an activity, but I never spoke harshly or became cross with any of them. Being totally and pleasantly surprised by this remarkable phenomenon, I sometimes reported the blessing to other adults.

Invariably they'd ask, 'No cross words in all this time? How come?'

Fair question, I thought, and my response always ran along these lines: 'The kids are just a pleasure to be with and to teach at all times.'

Then I'd hear, 'Well! That's just extraordinary. You wouldn't go five minutes with most kids without having some disciplinary problem. Why then are the Weabonga children so good? Are they angels?'

I always answered the same way. 'No, these are ordinary kids. They're just good kids. Not angels. They show me that any ordinary kid, anywhere, can be delightful.' As some folk, really intrigued by my claims, pushed me further, I'd add, 'Not every child, even given all the support and assistance, and living with the same expectations, will be as well behaved as the children are with me at Weabonga.' That required further explanation, so I'd add, 'All the conditions of nurture align for the Weabonga children. I know that won't be the case for every child. But, I believe, given best support and facilitation, most children can develop as happy, cooperative and respectful.

These Weabonga children are helping me become optimistic about the potential for all children.'

Why my pupils were so easy and rewarding was a question I had frequently asked myself. Indeed, I'd been asking myself questions about behaviour and discipline since day one at the school. On the first Saturday in Weabonga, while inspecting the school and going through the stores, I'd come across a Punishment Book. This was an official record book in which to register my use of corporal punishment, and its discovery made me reflect on the unlikely use of any caning in this little bush school. I was disconcerted that someone had covered the book with flowery wallpaper. Which teacher of the past had attempted to reduce the horror of this register by hiding its reality?

At Kegworth, there had been three classes in a General Activities (GA) section. GA schooling was designed for those pupils of post-primary age who, it was judged, couldn't cope with an academic curriculum at high school but still had to be held in school until the legal leaving age. The GA pupils at Kegworth were all teenage lads, and I thought they seemed disaffected, unmotivated and alienated. I'd been glad I didn't have to teach those youngsters. The four experienced teachers assigned to the GA classes created and modelled a harsh regime, believing they were containing the lads through the frequent daily use of corporal punishment. Each GA teacher possessed a cane, and two carried a cane with them at all times, only putting them aside when in the staffroom.

This approach to 'instruction' had reminded me, miserably, of the 'schooling' that had revolted me and against which I'd eventually rebelled when I suffered with the Christian Brothers during my own high school years. At that institution, rather than canes they wielded straps: instruments made from two strips of leather, each about two inches wide and eighteen inches long. Between these leather pieces a length of metal was introduced, and the three were stitched together with a thick, raised cord. This created a formidable weapon capable of delivering severe pain to any lad who couldn't remember the full conjugation of the Latin verb 'to love'.

'*Amo, amat.*'

'Hold out the left hand.'

Thwack. Flinch.

'Now, again.'

'*Amo, amaert.*'

'Hold out your right hand.'

Thwack, thwack, thwack. Flinch, flinch, huge flinch. But no matter what, don't express pain, and, please God, don't cry.

All would watch the culprit's hand swell up and glow an orangey-red—relief sought, perhaps, by stuffing the throbbing appendage under armpits or shaking it with vigour.

All Catholic schools permitted corporal punishment, but Christian Brother teachers had a reputation for being unrelenting floggers, worse than most. They wielded the strap in almost every lesson, never just a gentle tap but unrestrained belting. In my experience, most Brothers deliberately used their full strength to deliver real pain to the unfortunate lad holding out his hand. It seemed the Brothers believed if it was going to happen it might as well happen properly. No point otherwise.

The state also allowed the use of canes for corporal punishment in their schools. Alongside the Punishment Book in the Weabonga storeroom I had found an order book for replenishing Department of Education supplies: inks, nibs, exercise books. When I'd flicked through it I'd been surprised to find I could order, by sets of ten, a supply of canes. Of course, I'd known canes were frequently applied in public high schools. Supposedly, all use of canes had to be recorded in the official register like the one I was holding—but my friends who'd attended state high schools assured me little of their punishment had ever been recorded. All high school boys, not just my Christian Brothers classmates, had learnt to accept daily physical assaults as a rite of passage in their educational journey. Brave and unflinching lads had come to be admired by the rest of us. A few foolish but courageous boys defied their teachers to give them more 'cuts'. Secondary school could approach open warfare, and that had certainly often been the case in mine.

My fervent pledge had been never to treat a child as I'd been treated by those so-called Christian Brothers, but to surround kids with positive, supportive learning environments. It had distressed me to witness the treatment of the Kegworth GA boys—teenagers just like me when I was teaching there at the time—in what I thought should have been a calm atmosphere designed to assist them to repair and learn what they hadn't yet mastered.

I was never going to hit the Weabonga children, I had decided, no matter what. So, before I'd met them I'd decided I would support and facilitate their development, as much as I could, through gentle encouragement. Since then I'd kept an open eye on them, expecting to encounter some inappropriate activities. I never did. I found no reason at all to punish any of them.

By nature, the children were their families' offspring, I had no doubt. But I wondered: had they inherited their admirable qualities or learnt them from their families and the environment in which they were raised? Nature versus nurture had often been debated during my teacher training and is still hotly debated by scientists today. I just knew that the children's calm and equable approach to life had developed in their homes before they'd come to me.

23

June Baulderstone and Monica Whitworth, village mums, always came to our Parents and Citizens meetings, held monthly on a school day after 3.30 p.m., and Vic Teegan came often, whenever he could. We couldn't schedule meetings for later in the evening as parents stressed that this would be too intrusive on their family lives and work. On a few occasions we were joined by the women's husbands, Max and Bill, with whom I'd done some shearing work at the Williamsons'.

In reality we had little to discuss at these meetings, their greatest achievements being the raffle to purchase the record-player, and the physical organisation behind our annual concerts. But it was important for us to share a chat now and then, and keep track of how everything was going at the school. The P and C group provided an excellent sounding-board, and I checked many of my decisions with them. Unfailingly, I met with genuine support. The parents were delighted I was throwing myself into giving their kids a sound education, so they wanted me to feel appreciated. The meetings also provided a vehicle for parents to raise any matter with me they wished; they rarely did so.

For me, these parents were a wonderful source of information about the kids, when something couldn't be obtained from the children's spontaneous descriptions of themselves and their families. The children had already revealed lots about their home lives, so I'd gathered titbits about the parenting they received, and what I'd heard had impressed me with its soundness and sense. It was good to hear more from the parents themselves.

June, Monica and Vic told me lots of intriguing facts about their own upbringing in the 1930s and '40s. Now, they advised me, they were following in their parents' footsteps.

I also had occasional chances to chat with Max and Bill. Some afternoons as I left the school, I'd come across the two of them talking together at the roadside, and they'd often invite me to join in their discussion. We'd squat on our haunches at the roadside bank.

Max was the older of the two, by about eighteen months. He and June were raising their kids in a weatherboard cottage near the timber bridge over the Swamp Oak Creek. This was the original Baulderstone family home, the house in which Max and his three sisters, one of whom was now Monica Whitworth, had grown up. So, Max and Bill were brothers-in-law. Bill and Monica were raising their sons in the old police station house.

Two other Baulderstone sisters lived elsewhere; they had married and moved to reside well away from the village. The four siblings now found it difficult to come together at any one time and place. Max and Monica regretted this, as all four had been very close as youngsters.

After the original Baulderstone parents died, the family home had gone to Max, the eldest. Property in the Weabonga village wasn't necessarily valuable, but for him it was a life saver to have inherited a home of his own.

Bill and Max were best mates. Max said to me on one occasion, 'We're real close. I can rely on Bill, and he knows I'm always here if needed.'

Bill added, 'Yeah. We're like the fingers and the glove.'

The Whitworth home in the old police station was quite substantial and had a useful addition: a lock–up cell at the rear. This was now a storeroom, although Bill sometimes pretended to frighten his boys with a comical threat if they'd been a bit naughty. 'I'll lock you up and lose the key,' he'd growl. Bill said both his boys recognised this as a joke but went along with it by pleading for their dad's forgiveness. This bit of play talk allowed Bill, so he said, to discuss the boys' behaviour with them and to explain what was required of them. This wasn't unusual for Weabonga parents: I heard that many discussed their expectations of the kids quite openly with them. The village men's friendly and supportive relationship with their kids was a characteristic I'd noted of all local families.

Max and Bill had a pleasant approach to the world, being relaxed and even–tempered whenever I saw them. They seemed happy to be who they were and just accepted others as they came. They liked a joke and laughed often. Occasionally they took a shot at me, as they had sallied during the Williamsons' shearing week, but it was done gently, with a clear inference that no malice was intended. In fact, I was happy to field their digs, as I interpreted them as a mark of respect. Max and Bill had formed an impression of me and judged, I thought, that I was a down-to-earth bloke who would go along with some well-intended chiacking and give back as good as I got. They were pretty right—nothing they ever said or did raised my hackles, and I found our late afternoon confabs, hunkering on our heels at the roadside, genuinely interesting and companionable.

As we talked we had the occasional cigarette. I was a smoker, as was most everyone I knew, and my choice was for a tailor-made, untipped cigarette in a packet of twenty. I never smoked when at the school and only had five or six cigarettes over the day. I limited my smoking to reduce costs.

Bill and Max rolled their own. If I offered them a tailor-made, which I did often, they never took it, even though my smokes were untipped and unfiltered as were those they preferred, and they never offered me their pouch. They were expert at rolling a fag—never before had I seen such meagre smokes as they created. I thought of them as racehorses: thin, little thoroughbreds. Whenever shreds of tobacco escaped the paper before the men lit up, they would pinch these threads out and carefully return them to the pouch. Not one shred of tobacco was ever wasted. From those thin fags I understood they were more aware than I of the price of smoking. As each man talked, a skinny fag would hang off the corner of his mouth, bobbing up and down in a little dance.

Our afternoon talks ranged freely over many topics and could take off in any direction, mostly being idle chatter. These were rambling, natural conversations—just men's stuff. But after a while, some themes emerged. These talks helped me understand that most Weabonga parents shared a common experience and a common, present-day approach to child-rearing. Most of them, including Bill and Max, had been born in the mid-1920s or a little later, just prior to the onset of the Great Depression.

If I asked, all the parents would tell me of their experiences growing up at that difficult time. Clearly the Weabonga families of the 1930s and '40s had experienced poverty, worry and fear, and become even more isolated than previously. It was common to hear, 'We were only kids then, Pete. We just thought the way we were raised was normal. We thought that's how it was for everybody.' That was a message I had from them all, whether raised on a farm or in the village. No family was spared.

Looking back, all present-day parents said they could see how hard the times were for their own parents. Tony Wallace, a grazier, told me, 'My dad said that the price he got for our wool halved from 1929 to 1930 and then halved again in the next twelve months. We had to shear the sheep—you couldn't just let them go. By 1932, though, we weren't even clearing enough for the wool to pay the station's costs. We were going broke.'

Each village family, then as now, had about a half-acre around the family cottage: enough for a vegetable garden, a chook pen and some fruit trees, but not enough for stock. All the village families had some sheep and a few steers, though, running on the common. Each family subsisted partially on such produce.

Any income, though, then and now, came from the village men taking work on rural properties at any job that was offered, and all were totally dependent on this work to keep their families. Even the farm-owning parents had taken any work that became available. No one knocked back an opportunity to make a bit of cash throughout the Great Depression or for a long time following.

Max said his dad had been a gun shearer and all-round farm-hand. He could build and mend anything, so he'd had always had work—but not from 1929 onwards. The Baulderstone family suffered like all the rest. 'Yeah, Dad was a hard worker. A real grafter. All the graziers round about preferred him. If he was available they'd give work to Dad first. So he was always busy. The Williamsons, the Clarks, and the Blacks, on the farms just down the road there, they had him with them a lot.' But during the Depression, 'Dad was around the home more often. We just saw more and more of him.'

'Look, Teach,' another local parent told me, 'Dad was a real okay bloke. He had always been a happy and easy-going fella. Always up for a laugh and a practical joke. But gradually he became quieter, much quieter. And then he became silent. He didn't crack jokes or play around with us much anymore.'

If any of them asked their mum what was happening, she would say, 'Let your dad be. Don't pester him. He's got a lot of worries on his mind.'

Bill explained that he and all the Whitworth kids knew their mum and dad loved and cared for them, so they listened and let up on their dad.

Max added, 'Of course, it was the same with us. With our dad working less there must have been less money coming into the house. But we never saw money so we didn't really understand what Mum and Dad were facing.'

The same message, that money was scarce or non-existent in the Great Depression, was spelt out to me by all the present-day parents, whether they were village residents or farm families.

'Pete, we never went anywhere. Never went much beyond the village. Never went to a shop. We had no need of money as kids. We never bought anything. The hotel was still going but there was nowhere for kids to spend money in this place. So having no money was just the way it was.'

As I listened, over some time, a disturbing picture emerged from their stories.

'Let me tell you, we never were really hungry. We ate what was put in front of us, but sometimes there wasn't much on our plate.'

'We never saw a baker's loaf of bread. That would'a cost fourpence then, and our mum couldn't spare that sort of money.'

'Dad made it clear there was no fussy eating in our home. We ate what was there. If we didn't eat we went to bed hungry. Dad said that was our choice.'

'Sometimes a pumpkin and nettle stew was all there was, a sort of soup. Sometimes Mum would put a potato or some rice in—that's if she had any. But we never said that we wanted something different. Dad made sure we always thanked our mum for the meals she provided.'

Intrigued, I asked, 'Nettles? How'd they taste?'

'Just like spinach when boiled up. Okay, I guess. And Mum said they were brim full of good things. Maybe she was having us on just to get us to eat. But we believed her and we ate them up.'

I'd noticed nettles spread about in almost every paddock. Paul later explained to me that they grew most profusely where sheep had been. They thrive on sheep manure and are spread by sheep as they move about the pastures, so nettles remained a source of greens for the Weabonga families throughout the Depression.

'You've got to understand, meat was a bit of a rarity. Dad would sometimes chop off a rooster's head and then we'd have a slap-up meal. Good memories.'

Monica said, 'Some of the graziers were good to us. The Williamsons would drop off a quarter of lamb if they had killed. They were really decent folks. Not all were as thoughtful as that.'

Each mother had simple recipes, attempts to feed a family with little expenditure: puftaloons, drop scones, johnnycakes, damper.

Bill told us one time, 'Dad said if you had to be broke then Weabonga was a good place for it.'

'Why?' I asked.

'Simple, mate. We can grow our own food. You can't do that in the city, can you?'

All the present-day dads told about becoming rabbit trappers as soon as they were able in the 1930s. All had understood this was necessary to help their families, and they were keen to do so and proud that they could.

'Everyone was trapping rabbits. Soon there were none left around the village. We had to find new places to set traps. But our dad was strict—we couldn't set traps on other people's land without permission. Dad said we always had to do the right thing. We had to obey all the laws and never trespass.'

'Yeah, he was stern. Always stuck to his guns, got him into a spot of bother sometimes. But, jeez, he was always fair. Fair to us, and fair to his neighbours.'

'But, by gee, he had us under control. "Stand up straight," he'd say. "Hold that knife and fork properly, and never speak with your mouth full. Mind your manners. No slouching here."'

'He was so honest as well. Everyone said you could rely on what our dad said. Mightn't like it sometimes but you could rely on it. He'd give his word and keep it. We learnt a lot from that.'

No matter which dad or mum was the focus of such a story, all the present-day parents spoke in the same way. Strong values had been shared among all the 1930s and '40s Weabonga families. Everybody was law abiding; everyone was reliable as far as they could be. Everyone was respectful and respectable. They helped each other if they could, and they kept their eye out for any family having greater difficulty.

As they got older, by the time they were nine or ten in the middle to late 1930s, the kids understood things were really tough. They had to grow up fast—the realities couldn't be hidden.

All of them worked on the home gardens, and all foraged for bush and wild foods: blackberries, edible native leaves, watercress in the creek, nettles and mushrooms. All monitored the fruit trees scattered around the village. Many goldminers' cottages had disappeared, but the trees they'd planted were still producing. But all said, 'You had to be bloody quick. Everyone had their eye out for any food around.'

I was confronted by how difficult it became for the families when I heard about the way they cleaned their teeth. Max told me, 'I told ya that grey box was a great, fine-burning wood. Yeah! Well, we used to gather the white ash from the fireplace, put it on a rag, then clean our teeth.'

Clothing must have been a continuous problem. June said, 'As children we grew not to care about looking smart.' They all seemed to enjoy telling me about the strange things they'd worn.

'We always had the arse out of our strides. Even our best going-to-school duds.'

'Yeah, Mum would patch them. She'd sew a patch on a patch. There was an old pair of Dad's moleskins she kept for cutting up. In the finish our duds had no original cloth, just moleskin patches.'

'But, Pete, all the kids' pants were the same. All hand-me-downs. All patched. No kid better than any other. Even the farm kids had patched trousers.'

'Gosh, we were all in it together. We all stopped noticing. You just looked the other way and said nothing so as not to embarrass anyone. Everyone just turned a blind eye.'

Some of the women, even though a bit hesitant, told me, 'Our mum couldn't keep buying panties for us so she made some out of flour bags.'

'Yep,' another woman would state, 'flour bags were white calico. Made up into quite serviceable knickers.'

'Remember needing shoes to go to school?'

'My God, yes. How could you forget? School was the only place we wore shoes. The teacher wouldn't let us attend unless we had shoes. It was a matter of safety, our Sir said.'

'The soles of our feet were like rhino hide. We could have walked across fire. We preferred bare feet. No way that our mum could afford new shoes, so we looked after the boot leather on the shoes we had. We wore shoes as little as we could and went barefoot most of the time.'

'Sometimes, if we were outside on a frosty winter morning we'd put our bare feet into fresh cow dung. That'd get them warm again.'

So the picture was clear: the present-day parents had grown up in desperate times. Nothing was easy, and things didn't become more comfortable until the early 1940s. All, including children, hopped in to help, families cooperated to relieve real suffering, and decent standards were maintained. The Great Depression is said to have ended about 1932, but the Weabonga residents didn't see that. Living stayed tough for the families all through the 1930s and on into World War II.

24

As a young fellow I was still working on questions of my place in the world, as well as broader questions about society's formation, structures and driving forces.

My rugby scene was composed mostly of young men with a rural and private school background, and some budding professionals and businessmen. I never met another teacher in that rugby competition, nor did I meet a clerk, tradesman, shearer, labourer or any everyday working man through rugby. This crowd wasn't a representative cross-section of country town society.

A few rugby supporters seemed to me to rather enjoy feeling separate from the general population, and I became interested in the way this country community organised itself. Life there wasn't the same, in quite striking ways, as the life I'd experienced in the city.

In New England I'd become aware of widespread recognition of several families whose contribution to the area was acknowledged as important and worthy. These families had been early settlers, squatters really, who had moved into the district as it was opening up to white settlement from the 1840s onward. Well-known families included the Whites, of the Saumarez and Booloominbah properties near Armidale, and the Gidley Kings, who settled the vast Goonoo Goonoo Station near Tamworth. Such families had, over a number of generations, come to be identified as the 'squattocracy'. That term wasn't always applied positively, as it had connotations of the aristocracy and was associated with pretensions better left behind in England—although I saw no indications that the Whites or the Gidley Kings deserved any negative judgements.

The means by which the squattocracy had obtained land intrigued me. I wondered, had these families come to any kind of accord with the Aboriginal people they had displaced? These Anglo-Irish families had settled on the most productive land in the region, so I assumed it had been the country of a significant number of Aboriginal people. But in 1960, I never heard anyone question the legitimacy of the white occupation of the land.

My O'Brien forebears had themselves been among the early settlers in New England. Driven from Ireland by economic necessity, upon arrival in the late 1870s my grandparents had travelled straight from the ship at Circular Quay to the Tenterfield area and settled on an acreage some fifteen miles to the east of the town, in the Black Swamp area, towards the direction of Drake. Gradually they had converted pristine scrub and forest into pasture land. In order to establish an income, my O'Brien grandfather had, with a horse, dray, pick and shovel, taken contracts to build and maintain roads in the area. How, though, they had acquired title to their farm I had never enquired and had never been told as far as I could remember. I'd simply assumed it had been purchased, but the reality was probably that their settlement and ownership had been legitimised through the Land Acts of the 1860s: if a white person settled and worked the land, and added improvements, they might obtain the title.

As their family grew, my grandparents became concerned about the lack of educational opportunities for the children. A decision was made to sell the farm and move to Sydney, where they established their dairy—a trade they well understood from Ireland—in Edgecliff and Double Bay, and their children started school in Paddington.

Vague memories remain of a holiday I spent in Tenterfield when I was of primary school age, visiting and staying in the homesteads of grazing properties held by old Irish family friends of my dad: the Moran, Petrie and Connolly families in particular. I also remembered visiting one day the site of the timber cottage built by my grandad on country to the east of Tenterfield town; there was nothing of it left except the rough, grassy outline of the original foundations.

From that history I had an understanding of and sympathy for the dignity and worth some bestowed on these New England pioneering families. Starting from nothing, and by huge physical endeavours and merciless persistence, they had built a life for their families, a community with their neighbours and an infrastructure for their society. So there was something valuable to accept about them and much to admire. However, I disagreed when some in the rugby crowd went further than simply accepting the worth of such families and acted as though they were superior to others.

⌒

In my second year with the club, a need arose to appoint a new First Grade captain. One candidate stood out. Roy was marvellous; he had played in the Drummoyne First Grade team in the Sydney competition and been selected for the national Barbarian team playing against the visiting British Lions—the Barbarians were just outside selection for the Australian test team, so Roy was good. He understood rugby; he was a great tactician and strategist, and a fiery but absolutely fair and unrelentingly strong player. A leader on the field, he was always encouraging his team to do their best and lifting them when needed. Roy was the obvious next captain.

But rumours and criticism began to spread among the local rugby crowd. 'He lacks polish.' 'How would he perform when speech making if called on to represent the club?' 'He's too rough a diamond.'

Roy, an insurance salesman, was well liked by all his clients, even if his speech was a little unpolished. But he wasn't appointed to the captaincy. The whispering campaign, well managed, denied him what should rightfully have been his. Roy took it all with grace. Appointed in his place was a private school–educated businessman, a reasonable club-standard player, with far less rugby knowledge and skill than Roy, little charisma and few leadership qualities.

Such attitudes challenged me. What was going on with these 'born to rule' folk? I certainly didn't believe that superiority could be obtained by birthright or any unearned privilege. I was disconcerted and quite troubled by the attitudes I was now witnessing, and the rights seemingly reserved for only some of those with whom I was interacting.

One of my college lecturers had discussed the social origins of teachers. He rather upset my sectional peers when he claimed that young male entrants to the teaching profession came, typically, from the 'upper working class', while typical female entrants came from the 'lower-to-middle middle class'. He suggested male school leavers entered teaching as a means to progress up the class scale, while females used teaching to ensure they didn't slip down the social scale.

Inwardly I considered my origins and those of my college peers. I guess most of us took a surreptitious look around. There were no professional families represented by me or any fellow student. As the lecturer suggested, all of us were from 'lower social classes', as far as that concept had any meaning in Australia. When I glanced at my peers, I saw fine young people eager and keen to become excellent teachers—all supportive, kind, pleasant if not charming, and bright of wit. I didn't care to what class, if any, they belonged. They were wonderful just for whom they were. If there were 'right people', they were certainly pretty right. Besides, I told myself, my entry to teaching was for the pursuit of knowledge, not climbing up a class ladder.

Apart from a few years on the family farm in New England, my father had been a minor public service manager. He had left his Darlinghurst school when he was fifteen and, having joined a government department as his first paid job, stayed with that department for his entire working life. He had grown up in a home near his family's dairy farm in Sydney's Double Bay, with their herd pastured on an area now known as the Lough Playing Fields, off Manning Road. The O'Brien family's original stone-built dairy remained in place, on a corner site of the Fields, disguised as a service station. My dad's boyhood home was up the hill some way from the dairy property, one of the group of four large cottages that together made up The Grove, a housing enclave off Queen Street, Woollahra. One of his tasks as a teenager had been to mow, roll with a heavy hand-roller and apply lines to the grass tennis court attached to his home.

That O'Brien home was the first house I entered in my life. My grandparents still lived in it when I was born, and on her way home from the maternity hospital my mother stopped by and took me in to 'show me off'. I have no memory of either O'Brien grandparent, unfortunately, but from family stories I know they were decent folk with little formal education, earning their living from hands-on dairy work as small-business proprietors.

My mother came from a village and farming background in Ireland. She had only six years of schooling—a curtailment to her education forced on her by circumstances. As a girl it had become far too risky for her to continue her daily walk along the country backroads to the Castlepollard or Ballymacarney school. At the time of her sixth and final year, the British, who ruled the country, had unleashed on a fractious Ireland, desperate for independence, a paramilitary force about 6000 strong, known as the Black and Tans. Their main task, it seems, was to subdue the Irish population through terror. Irish girls and young women were considered fair game by the British thugs.

When I applied for an Irish passport to enable me to travel freely in Europe, I had to supply my mother's birth certificate in order to prove my lineage. I was shocked to note my grandfather had signed with an X. He had been the head herdsman for the Earls of Longford, the aristocratic title of the Pakenham family, and responsible for all the stock on the estate of the Pakenham family seat at Tullynally Castle near Castlepollard in County Westmeath. My grandfather was, so the story went, a noted judge of horses and cattle, and for these abilities he was held in great respect throughout the county. One entitlement in his work was to a house on the estate, so my mother grew up in a quite substantial two-storey home. She and all three of her siblings were literate, as was my grandmother. The reasons for my grandfather's lack of literacy are hard to fathom now.

My heritage is mixed but, clearly, there was no professional background on either side. If class was an issue, to which level or class did I belong from my jumbled family tree? I remembered my mother insisting that Australia was a classless society: one of its clear attractions for her. If she had been comparing it with the Ireland she had left in 1923, as an eighteen-year-old, she'd been correct.

My family and my schooling, particularly with the lovely nuns of my primary school, had influenced me greatly, of course, but I was trying to think through my interpretation of society independently and had developed a strong egalitarian model. It seemed to me that individual success and social standing were achieved through personal effort and endeavour. No one I had seen had won rewards or been recognised simply because of the perceived superiority of their birth or class. Superiority had to be earned.

I admired the accomplishments of individuals. Sometimes, though, I saw that a helping hand could produce quicker and more immediate rewards. So, I'd developed a philosophy of self-help with care for others thrown in. Early conversion to the acceptance that all are equal, not only in the sight of God—as taught to me by the nuns—but also manifestly to each other made me more egalitarian. I argued for the greatest good for the greatest number rather than a focus on self or of letting the devil take the hindmost.

By the time I arrived in Weabonga, I felt no need to play out someone else's class-based fantasy. All were equal, so I accepted everyone as I found them and as they treated me, and tried to treat others with respect and friendship whenever possible.

⌣

In the New England rugby scene, I met folk who challenged my ideals. A collection of men from rural 'leading families', aligned with businessmen from the region's towns, appeared to control power and its use in the region.

I was not surprised to observe such a group. During the years of my upper high schooling I'd noted men from my Kensington church combining with like-minded others from surrounding parishes to counteract the influence of communism in the Labor Party and the labour unions. They were part of 'the Movement', a semi-secret society founded and led by Bob Santamaria, a lay Catholic, with support from Archbishop Daniel Mannix, the rather fiery Irish prelate of Melbourne. 'The Movement' had become a significant force, advocating an exaggerated traditional form of Catholicism and a heightened conservativism in politics.

My older brother spent several nights a week working with the organisation and, despite its requirement of secrecy, had divulged some aspects of it to me. I didn't find them appealing. Even as a teenager I believed that if such objectives were worthy, they should be reached by more legitimate means—such as openly joining the Labor Party and taking an active part in its pre-selections, while publicly rebutting ideas and policies one might oppose. I perceived 'the Movement', with its hint of martyrdom, as a rather unsophisticated, 'church-in-peril' response to an exaggerated threat. And I pooh-poohed one of Santamaria's more curious suggestions: to settle all Australian families on small rural selections, in order to promote their ability to become partially self-supporting, as in a seventeenth-century Italian state. Now, when I saw how successful such a model was in helping to raise the bonny Weabonga children, I had to admit a little grudging respect. That didn't make the idea feasible, though, throughout most of late twentieth-century Australia.

A few years later, while in the National Service with university men, I had been approached by associates of the Eureka Youth League. I had no doubt they were trying to recruit me. Openly associated with the Australian Communist Party, Eureka claimed to be working for social justice and the rights of all, particularly the young. Such goals appealed to me, and some of their events might have been fun. For a brief moment I considered a loose association, but then I realised that Eureka was too similar to 'the Movement' for me. Both demanded strict adherence to their modes of thinking, believing and acting. I sought a more individualistic answer to many of life's questions, finding my way to a truer, more personal interpretation of society.

Even though I rejected 'the Movement' and Eureka, I viewed each as working for their version of the greater good. Here in New England, though, I observed a group organising for what I perceived to be the pursuit of narrow sectional or even just selfish interests. But, to my surprise, these New Englanders were quite successful in capturing social and political power.

I asked my local acquaintances and friends to explain how such people, 'born to rule', apparently uninterested in and even dismissive of those they considered inferior—most people, it seemed—came to wield such influence, especially when many of the positions they held were electable. 'Easy,' was the response. 'The squattocracy and nabobs have control of decisions that affect people's lives. They employ people, either through their rural holdings, through the town-based businesses into which they've invested, or through their influence on the shire councils. Many people owe them a living. Casting a vote the right way is an attempt by an elector to curry their favour.'

No one suggested there was any corruption in place. Votes weren't being bought but, nevertheless, debts could be brought in, if only by implication, and the application of hints and indirect pressure.

The 'nabob' operations were well illustrated by their very active, well-organised and well-funded campaign to have New England recognised as a separate state. Prominent in this advocacy to secede were a few names from the squattocracy, with many others from the leading businessmen. The editor of the Tamworth-based newspaper, the *Northern Daily Leader*, gave them access to a powerful means of communicating their push for statehood.

In my assessment, any such new state would need subsidisation forever from the mother state, New South Wales, and be an eternal drag on the economies of both that state and the nation. In trying to build support, the New England state advocated that the Newcastle and Hunter Valley areas be included in the new state. But the Hunter people had no interest whatsoever in leaving New South Wales or in joining a New England. It was clear to most that a push for a New England state based on the inclusion of the Hunter was absolutely doomed to failure from the outset. But such a failure wasn't apparent to the nabobs who led the push.

Questions about the underlying motivation for this new state movement kept arising in my mind. Clearly it wasn't in the best interests of Australians generally, nor even of those living in the region. From what and from where, I wondered, came this dream and the intense efforts being expended on its unlikely achievement? That personal needs for aggrandisement and individual desires for power were at play, as much as anything, appealed to me as a likely explanation. Could it have been a case of a big fish in a much smaller pond? Personal desires were outgunning public good, I concluded.

I did wonder how it was that the regional leadership, which claimed to be working in the best interests of country people, seemed to have so little concern for the lives led by those I knew, such as the good folk of Weabonga. Many other public and social goals might have better qualified for support from the power, knowledge and vitality of the 'right people' than a new state. If the nabobs were looking for causes to champion, I thought they may have been helped by paying a visit to our isolated little village and hearing a few suggestions.

At our one-teacher bush school we might have discussed the lack of electricity, and the schoolroom being unsupplied with illumination, a radio, musical instruments or a moving-picture projector. We might have discussed the lack of running water and sewerage. We might have discussed the limited reading material and the absolute dearth of reference books when city schools had libraries. We might have discussed the lack of music, arts and crafts materials when town and city schools had speciality rooms, materials and teachers. We might have discussed the fact that these country children had no visit from medical or dental services in my two years when students at all town and city schools did at least annually. We might have discussed the lack of counsellors and careers advisers. We might have discussed the typical teaching appointment of inexperienced, barely competent young men, like me, to these little, isolated schools. We might have discussed why it was that rural children weren't receiving equal educational opportunities to children in towns and cities.

Provision of decent education for country children everywhere was—I thought—worth fighting for.

But the nabobs might have responded by charging me with the promotion of my own narrow sectional interest: while there were many small bush schools in New England, their supporters represented relatively few voters. To counteract any such accusation, I would have introduced the new staters to Ethel and Perc, who, in their own forthright way, would have mentioned road and communication needs, the upgrading of hospitals, the provision of decent health care in smaller rural communities, and the connection, at last, of electricity and adequate sewerage throughout New England. To me, my elderly friends had a more insightful grasp of local priorities than any of the new staters.

I had little doubt whose interests the nabobs were truly promoting. They made me somewhat cynical about the use of political power in rural Australia. It's always sensible, I believed, to dig deep into the motives of anyone making appeals for the support of country people.

I remained happy to be part of the hoi polloi. My view of all men being equal was strengthened. I was certain the idea of social class, if it existed, mattered not at all to me, and I should just let it waltz by.

With the people I saw most frequently, the residents of Weabonga, my expectations of society were met. I understood them. They provided a necessary balance, showing the inherent worth and decency of ordinary people. All the men were extremely hardworking, whether graziers or labourers. All the women, whether from homestead or village cottage, were devoted to their families and spent long, long hours in caring for them. No distinctions were made that I ever saw. Everyone worked diligently at achieving the goals they set themselves, and often a friendly, helping hand was offered about. Weabonga people had reached out to alleviate my distress and give me support. I appreciated and was happy to take part in the genuine society they created together.

More importantly, the children in our little bush school—through their fondness for each other, in their ongoing, unconditional support for their schoolmates, and by their own efforts—modelled a fine society.

I was fortunate that much of my country life was fulfilling and my social life fun, so the squattocracy and nabobs didn't count for much to me. My crowd of local friends worked hard but also found time to enjoy themselves. Most were progressing sensibly toward important, solid goals, not wasting time and effort on pies in the sky. Most were planning on marriage—and I was beginning to think of doing the same.

⁓

Marriage planning had been brought to my attention in a curious way.

Within a month or two of meeting, Patricia and I had established a semi-regular pattern of going on outings. At first, any conviction that our outings were actually dates eluded me. I hadn't formed any serious intention, although I enjoyed her company immensely and felt a growing interest. Her charming qualities impressed me.

When my twenty-first birthday came along, my family planned a simple celebration at home, to which they invited all my mates and other friends. My mother took care of the catering, along with Peg, her long-time friend.

Peg was a wonderful woman. Of Northern Irish background, she was a social powerhouse with a compelling singing voice well suited to heart-pulling Irish melodies. Her rendition of the 'Spinning Wheel', for example, was spine tingling, comparable in quality to any version I'd heard. Peg's husband, Barney, was her equal in joie de vivre. In the early 1920s he'd been an active member of the legitimate Irish Republican Army and, when it came his turn at a party, he could sing so strongly the rebel song 'The Old Fenian Gun' he might have moved mountains. Peg and Barney had been present throughout my life, and I enjoyed sharing my birthday with them.

Patricia had been invited, but not necessarily as a girlfriend. It was early days.

During the evening Patricia assisted by fetching and carrying food and drink from the kitchen. On one trip she overheard a comment Peg addressed to my mother: 'Mairy, thut guurl is go-un' to get yur Paytuh.'

Patricia said nothing to me on the night, but later revealed this episode to me on one of my Sydney trips. I apologised for any embarrassment and asked if she'd responded.

'Yes,' she told me, 'I said in turn, "But I may not want to catch your Peter."'

Admittedly, at the time of my birthday I wasn't yet ready to be caught, so I saw Patricia's response as reasonable. At twenty-one I hadn't begun to think seriously about marriage; while I had considered it, I'd acknowledged to myself I was too immature to take on such a responsibility. While at Weabonga, though, I'd started contemplating a married future, and I felt a little anxious that my chances with Patricia might have been knocked for six by Peg's indiscretion.

As my time at Weabonga and Patricia's in Melbourne extended, we depended more and more on our letters and phone calls to maintain and grow our friendship, which became increasingly meaningful and important for me. But conducting this long-distance romance wasn't easy. I was worried that Patricia had established herself so well in Melbourne—her 'rat pack' sounded very supportive—that she might not want to leave.

I was reassured that she made sure to come up to Sydney so we could spend time together when I had opportunities to visit from Weabonga. All the hours we spent talking on the phone and being together during holiday periods became charged for us both. The more I saw Patricia, the more I appreciated her. I recognised I had fallen in love and I loved the feeling. There was nothing better for me than being in love.

I believed my being teacher-in-charge at Weabonga was accelerating my emotional and intellectual growth. I began to think in a different way about our friendship, and the possibility of getting married came to figure in all my thoughts of the future. I now came to believe I was ready for commitment. But was this reasonable, I wondered? Was I, just through isolation and loneliness, imposing inappropriate feelings on the friendship? Was I overly dependent and taking advantage of the young woman's kindness? I didn't wish to place Patricia in a position where she might feel compromised and hemmed in by me and my needs. But, I reminded myself, I wasn't dependent on Patricia: several of the young women in my crowd in town had made it obvious they were willing to entertain ideas of a closer relationship with me. This went some way to convincing me that I wasn't imposing a personal need on my friendship with Patricia.

The other thing was that Patricia's ability to strike out in an independent manner, her confidence in her decisions, and her assertive behaviour when speaking up for herself had always impressed and delighted me. As I thought it through, I came around to believing she was quite capable of telling me any necessary home truths.

Encouraged, I made my feelings clearer in every letter and phone call. We moved closer to an important decision.

25

At the end of my first year at Weabonga, I travelled down to Sydney, Patricia came up from Melbourne, and we spent lots of time together over the Christmas period. Her grandparents welcomed me to a festive meal on Boxing Day, and Patricia and I swam, picnicked and partied with my mates and their growing group of girlfriends. We had a wonderful week before she needed to return to her work in Melbourne.

For the remainder of the holiday I enjoyed a trip to Perth with a friend, Leo, visiting his older brother who had set up business there. The home where we stayed was right on Cottesloe Beach, and we enjoyed an almost perfect summer.

During this holiday, I purchased, for the right price, a small and relatively new two-door car, then drove it back to Sydney over the Nullarbor Plain. One advantage of teaching in an isolated school was that for the first time in my life I'd built up some savings.

Despite some hitches and excitement while covering such a distance on rough gravel roads, the little car got me back to Weabonga in time for the commencement of my second year as teacher-in-charge.

As I drove up to the school gate for the first time, the children excitedly ran beside me, shouting and calling.

But as I stepped out of the little two-tone, boxy brown vehicle, Joe Wallace made an announcement. 'You're driving a biscuit tin, Sir.'

I had to laugh. Of course, my biscuit tin made a huge difference to me. At last I could come and go from school exactly as I pleased, arriving as early and staying as late as I liked, without fear of impossible road conditions for motorbike riding. And it would be much easier for me to plan weekends in Tamworth and surrounds.

In six towns where I played rugby I had access to balls run by social organisations, variously called The Town and Country, The Black and White, and The Bachelors and Spinsters. Winter was the ball season, and I could have, if I'd wanted, attended twelve or so balls in a few months. In my second Weabonga year, with the help of my little car, I accepted six of the ball invitations. My dancing feet were back.

I could also slip down to Sydney more frequently. The little car was nippy, so I could do the run as well as anyone in much bigger motors. I would set off straight after school on Friday and be back in Weabonga late on Sunday evening, after two nights and most of two days in the city. I began to pick up on my friendships, particularly with Patricia, and to enjoy musical theatre productions and the concerts of visiting entertainers whom I would never get a chance to hear in the country.

Any outing with Patricia was, in my mind, no longer just an outing but a real date, with auguries of the future. We were both still relatively young, I being only just twenty-two, but by then I was fairly well smitten.

My positive experiences with my pupils were now having an impact on my thoughts. I resisted any notion that I was their parent—I clearly wasn't—but spending time with those delightful children eventually prompted me to think of having children of my own. And the thought of having them with Patricia was becoming somewhat irresistible to me even if not yet openly discussed between us. As we continued to share experiences, though, ideas for a possible shared future arose and were not summarily dismissed by either of us.

Patricia and I enjoyed music and attending performances together, especially when we could see celebrities visiting from overseas. We would see these international stars perform at the only venue large enough: the old boxing stadium at Rushcutters Bay.

We saw Frank Sinatra there. Frank appeared unhappy on the night and finished up after what seemed a brief set, certainly not worth anyone's money. Of course we were disappointed—this was Sinatra's first trip to Australia and we'd saved for the price of admission. At the time, we felt somewhat cheated. But we came to talk about Frank and his moods often, and joked about him in our phone calls and letters. 'Frank-incense' became a code between us if we were aiming to alert the other to a spot of displeasure when others were around.

After each Sydney break, my biscuit tin would take me quietly back up the highway, then off through the hills and up the Divide, to the village and our tiny school. I revelled in my new memories of joyful times with Patricia.

26

Wanting to reinforce the many positive qualities the children brought from their homes, I took opportunities to commend actions, discuss alternatives and sort out preferred ways of behaving. I encouraged the kids to talk about moral and ethical choices, even if we didn't call them that, and they were eager to express their opinions and help define acceptable conduct. Inevitably the children came down on the side of actions their parents and I would prefer they accepted. The younger children might just have been parroting and repeating the lessons from their parents—even so, I thought that a good start. The older ones, I believed, were coming to be characterised by their moral responses, and I thought that of huge potential benefit to them and the wider community.

Mr Flood only visited us once that second year. 'Peter,' he told me, 'I've seen much I truly like. Generally, things are continuing to go well. You've built on the fine start I saw last year, and the children seem to be learning well and progressing.

Everything appears in order. Your programs and attendance books are up to date and complete. The lesson plans you've shown me are exemplary.'

I felt a sound sense of relief—to be supported by an expert assessment was really heartening.

The inspector also emphasised the necessity for adherence to the set curriculum and the imperative to stick with the subject times identified. He added some suggestions, not calling any of them criticisms. Still, I took them to heart—one in particular.

'Peter,' he said, 'you must keep to the suggested timetabling reserved for religious studies. The curriculum is specific about that.' He added, 'I want you to think about the children's moral and ethical development. We must care for the children's all-round progress. Much help will come for them from the religious lessons you provide. Most of these children will never attend a church so they may not get much else about moral development except what you cover at school.'

Perhaps my inspector's emphasis on religion had arisen from a devout Christian background—possibly an adherence to the Baptist or Methodist faith, denominations much in control of the Department of Education at that time.

Putting his advice into the context of my experiences in Weabonga, I believed the inspector was selling our community short if he thought there wasn't parental and community concern for the children's moral development. School wasn't the only source of moral education, and neither were religious institutions. All the adults in Weabonga were keen to help the children develop as fine, brave, upright people.

I was somewhat resistant to this requirement to teach religious studies in our one-room school. At Kegworth, we everyday teachers hadn't engaged in religious education: it had been carried out by visiting voluntary teachers or catechists from several denominations. Each Thursday a period was set aside for these lessons, and the children would be withdrawn from their normal classes and grouped according to their faith designation. Unsurprisingly, all the Thursday visitors were Christian. There was no need for teachers of faiths such as Hinduism or Islam: no children from those backgrounds were enrolled in the school, and I wasn't aware of other faiths being taught at schools around about. According to the census, Australia was almost entirely a Christian society.

But there were no visitors to attend our little bush school, so, apparently, religious education was solely my responsibility.

Feeling quite unprepared to be leading the children at Weabonga in religious training of any sort, I still accepted that it must be addressed somehow in our school—the inspector and state required it. Proselytising or evangelism, though, wasn't my role.

～

Our Lady of Perpetual Succour, the small Catholic church in the village, was used on a monthly basis, with a mass conducted every fourth Sunday by a visiting priest. I attended once early in my time in Weabonga, joining a congregation of twelve parishioners: three families and me. Two farm families in attendance weren't known to me. Sue, from the post office, and her two boys, Jack and Steve, were also kneeling together in a pew. Alongside them knelt an older man. After the mass, I met the priest and all in the congregation, and was introduced by Sue to her dad, Tim. Apart from Sue and her boys, as well as Tim, with whom I did later come to be quite friendly, I never saw the other mass folk again.

That was my single attendance in that tiny church, as after that I was always away in Tamworth or on holidays at all other mass times. My absence was noted, and the visiting priest asked the congregation about my habits. More than six months later, Tim passed on these pastoral concerns. I'd expected them following my absences, as a parish priest has the responsibility for the eternal salvation of all his parishioners. His task is to ensure every member of his congregation succeeds in life's single important goal: a good death and an eternity in heaven. So I knew this one just wanted to 'save my soul'. I felt no resentment at his asking others about me, as I understood the genesis of his concern, but I let Tim know that I was prepared to take personal responsibility for my salvation and that he was free to let the priest know that.

Was I certain of salvation at the time? Not at all, and I wasn't being cocksure or disrespectful in my message to the concerned priest. In fact, I was far from certain. Was salvation even a real prospect? My beliefs were wavering as I got older. A lessening of my faith and diminishment of conviction about many things were two of the many changes occurring in me at Weabonga; I was far less persuaded of matters I had previously taken for granted, and more open to subtleties in interpretation and nuances in thought and belief about many aspects of life, not only religion.

St George's, the tiny Church of England in the village, had welcomed no visiting ordained minister and no services since 1954, and I saw little evidence that families journeyed to attend Sunday church services anywhere else. Aside from Jack and Steve at the Catholic chapel, only the two daughters of the lay-preaching dad, Lindie and Susie, attended any church service as far as I knew. Consequently I assumed that organised religion had only a small and indirect influence on most of my pupils' development of moral and ethical behaviour.

In my presence the parents didn't gossip or speak about other parents. Any discussion remained general in nature and positive in tone. On one occasion only I heard a somewhat disparaging remark from one parent about another. In the lay-preaching dad's absence, a parent referred to him as 'The Lie Preacher'. A slight smile accompanied the suggestion, a hint that the remark was meant to be more comical than critical. But it was a personal put-down, and I thought about its further meanings. The remark conveyed to me a somewhat negative view not only of the man but also about organised religion.

All the Weabonga families were ostensibly Christian, and I supported that religion as a sound source of morals and ethics, but I thought that other, more humanistic sources could be providing guidance and direction to the families. The Weabonga adults were fine, reliable people and their children were growing admirably. These traits were to be treasured and reinforced, whatever their wellspring.

All the children had been registered as having a Christian background—so, if I was to cover religion, I thought I'd be safe concentrating on Bible stories. At one P and C meeting I checked with my small committee, and they endorsed selecting appropriate sections from the Bible for religious instruction. There was no discussion or suggestion of any comparative studies of religion. Australia was a Christian country. With what might Christianity be compared?

The kids were always happy to talk about all they read or heard. Any understanding they took from their reading was batted back and forth between them as they nutted out what a story was truly about. Every story—from their *School Magazine*, from the books accumulating on the schoolroom shelf, from ABC Radio—was analysed and assessed.

I recalled an occasion when Charlie and Jimmy had been reading their primer out loud with me. The other pupils over-heard this reading and, for some reason, the storybook family piqued their interest. A conversation sprang to life.

'That dad went to work in an office. Our dads go to work with sheep in the paddocks all day. Our dads are outside all the time. In an office you'd be inside all the time. I wouldn't like that much.'

'Never been in an office. That would be rotten. In an office all day.'

'Yeah, but some dads mightn't be good at farm work. Maybe the dad in the story knew nothin' about sheep or cattle. You've gotta do what you're good at.'

'Suppose so, but I'd rather do what I like doin'. I like being out in the paddocks. That suits me.'

'Is that what you'll do when you get big?'

'Yeah. Sure. When I'm big I'll work on a farm to make some money to look after my kids.'

That interaction had centred on the boys, but the older girls, who'd been listening in, jumped into an opening.

'Wonder what the mum in that story did? Her husband was away in an office all day. What did she do? The story doesn't tell us.'

'Well, she'd have to look after her two kids, wouldn't she? Mums look after kids.'

'And that dad had a real white shirt, didn't he? Someone had to do the washing and ironing and keep the home clean and tidy. She'd have been busy as billy-oh.'

Chatter like that promoted broader discussion, and we might cover topics including the responsibilities and work lives of men and women, of mums and dads. Such conversations easily took in ethics and morals.

Tom might say, 'Who says dads go out to work and earn the money? Is that right?'

Vickie might then ask, 'Is it right that mums stay at home to look after kids?'

Each child spoke their mind and stated their beliefs.

Every idea would get an airing but, as I remember it, no radical suggestion ever got a guernsey. There was a robust interchange but mostly with a great deal held in common. And, without any surprise, that particular talk ended with an unstated but clear decision that men and women married and raised children together, with dads going to work and mums staying at home to look after kids. That was the correct and only way it was in our rural setting of 1961.

I felt sure I could find one suitable Bible story a week for the rest of the year, and this would meet the curriculum's requirements. I was pleased that this religious coverage would sit within a broader context in which morals and ethics were discussed whenever opportunities arose, no matter the timetabled title of the subject being studied at the time. I thought life shouldn't be separated into slots of time in which we practised being ethical then reverted to a lack of interest in right behaviour. I wanted the kids to know that all aspects of life required moral decisions, and I was confident they would learn to make sensible choices when faced with dilemmas.

I decided to select positive stories from which the children might draw guidance. So we read or heard stories of friendship and love, joy and kindness. Generally I avoided the Old Testament, and any stories laden with condemnation and punishment. These well-behaved children didn't need guilt, fright and terror. Goodness was present each day in our school: it came through the door with the children's arrival, and I wanted to reinforce and reward that.

Anything that included animals—the Lost Sheep, Noah's Ark—was hugely enjoyed. Animals were clearly part of God's creation. Asked to draw examples of a Bible story from their own life, the children would quickly cite parallels, at least in their minds, and many involved animals. And, unfortunately or not, these country kids knew the sad reality of the end for many animals.

Lindie and Susie shared in telling a story in response to the parable of the Good Samaritan.

'When we were coming back from the church at Bowling Alley Point last Sunday, we saw an injured roo at the side of the road.'

'He'd been hit by a car. Must have been the driver just in front of us.'

'The roo was still moving but couldn't get up. We were all upset. So Dad stopped the car.'

'Dad got out and went back to have a look. He said that the roo was too badly hurt.'

'He got the rifle from the car. He said he'd be a good neighbour and shoot the roo.'

'Dad was being kind. The roo was too hurt to get better. When he came back, Dad said he'd done the right thing.'

As enthusiastically as I could muster, I said, 'Well, yes. I guess that's being a good neighbour.' I couldn't quite work out whether the neighbour being assisted was the long-gone driver who'd done the original damage or the roo itself. In the minds of the children, animals were pretty close to people on the scale of priorities.

In response to the same story, Joe Wallace told us one morning, 'When Mum was driving us home after school yesterday we saw Clark's grader at the side of the road. It was in the same place as it had been when we passed it coming to school in the morning. Mum said she thought that was funny. She said, "We'll call in to Clark's—we pass their gate anyway—to see what's happened."'

Little brother Jimmy added quickly, 'Mr Clark said the battery from the grader had died. He was waiting for the mail car to bring a new battery from town. He'd have to wait a few days.'

Joe retook the story, 'My mum said we'd go and get the battery from our tractor and we'd bring it back and Mr Clark could get his grader going and then get it home off the side of the road.'

Jimmy rounded off the story. 'Mr Clark was happy. He thanked Mum. Then Mum said to him she was just being a good neighbour. "You've done the same for us, Mr Clark," Mum said.'

Around Easter in the second year, Vickie, Carol and Mark told us a truly moving tale, picking up on the message of Christ's giving his life to 'save' humankind. As was their wont, the three spread the telling between them. These joint narratives brought us glimpses of life in their hidden-away home, conveying the warmth and intimacy of their family—perhaps of an evening talking quietly together or playing simple card games, which the three siblings told us happened often in the lamplight.

Mark started this particular story. 'We were all sitting down to lunch on Saturday when we heard a big fuss in the yard. It was an awful big racket.'

One of his sisters jumped in. 'We all rushed out to see what was happening. There were chooks going crazy everywhere. Running around, clucking and squawking.'

'We could see Rusty, our red rooster, jumping up and down and crowing and calling out. He was fluttering up in the air and then he'd dive down.'

'He was real upset. He kept jumping up and down. All the chooks were calling out and running around. It was a real madhouse.'

'All the fowls were clucking and cackling, and Rusty was crowing like crazy.'

'We asked Dad what was happening, and he said Rusty must have spotted a snake.'

'Mum asked Dad to chase the snake away if he could. Dad went closer, but Rusty didn't stop.'

'Dad called out that he could see a big king brown and told Mum to take us inside. Dad said Rusty was trying to kill the snake but the snake was striking at Rusty whenever he came close.'

'We didn't see what happened next but the noise and clatter stopped.'

'From the door we asked Dad what was up.'

'Dad said not to come but he thought Rusty had been bitten by the snake. Dad said the snake had gotten away.'

'After a bit, Dad said we could come closer.'

'Rusty was lying still on the ground. He wasn't moving.'

'Mum asked, "Is Rusty dead?"'

'Dad said yeah. The snake had bitten and killed him.'

'We were all upset. Mark and Carol and me started crying, and Mum was crying a bit.'

'Dad said we should think of Rusty as a brave rooster. Dad said Rusty had died looking after his flock. He said Rusty was a champion and we should remember him that way.'

'We still are upset, though.'

What an impression that story made on us all. Every child was silent for a while—we'd been hearing stories of Rusty for a year or so, and we'd come to love the rooster as they did. We all said to Vickie, Carol and Mark how sorry we were.

Our teenager, Tom, commented, 'Only a rooster, but he died caring for the other chooks. He must have loved his hens. That's love no matter what.'

My inner voice was saying, *Good on you, Tom.*

27

I had learnt much about each child's family and home. It was clear early on that all the village dads were day labourers, taking jobs wherever they could find them in the local area. The three farm-based dads ran their own sheep properties, and were fully occupied in their pasture and animal management. All the fathers left home very early each morning, including sometimes on weekends, and returned late. The old advice to take advantage of daylight and work with the sun certainly applied to the Weabonga men.

If not out employed on a local property, the village dads spent the day near home, doing lots of heavy labour. Woodcutting was an ongoing need, summer or winter; the men scoured the country gathering limbs and logs to cut up for the wood stove in the kitchen, for the laundry copper, or for the fire in the grate needed in winter to keep the family warm. All these men were hard workers, diligent and reliable, grafting as well as they could to provide for their families.

Every mother stayed and worked at home, typical of women of that era. I knew of few married women anywhere who had employment outside of the home. But these country women had many chores and little in the way of appliances or support. Every chore, without exception, was done manually.

Monday was washing day. At each home, the morning began with the women filling a large copper and setting a fire in a grate beneath to heat the water. Bark scraps and sticks of wood were fed to the fire throughout the morning. Washing was done in batches: clothes, sheets, towels, coloureds and whites. The women had a sturdy stick to help them transfer washing from the copper to a tub. In the copper the washing was at boiling point, so touching it wasn't possible until it had been rinsed, item by item, in the tub in cold water. Using a mangle—the women turning its handle with the huge effort required—each tub load was wrung of as much water as possible. Setting the mangle with opposing wheels close together expelled most water although this made the job more demanding. Then the washing was ready to be hung out to dry. All the homes had long washing lines, and on Mondays each yard was festooned with whites and colours, each piece having been lifted and pegged in place separately.

Props kept the weighed-down lines above the ground. The men cut these props from the surrounding bush; they would carefully select a long, slender limb, then trim excess branches but retain an end branch to form a vee at the prop end. This shored up the whole line, allowing the washing to wave in a breeze. Lifting the line to place a prop required some strength and effort, but the women were adept at such labours. Washing took up the whole day and, if it had been fine and dry enough with a bit of a breeze, the washing could be collected and brought in, folded, at day's end. Monday must have been truly exhausting for each woman.

Tuesday was most often ironing day. With no electric power, in some homes the irons—literally just lumps of metal, or 'irons'—were stood to heat on top of the wood stove and lifted with a detachable handle that slotted into their heavy, solid metal bases. When an iron cooled down too much it was put back on the stovetop, and another heated iron took its place. These transfers had to be frequent, which meant an ironing board would be placed near the fire no matter the temperature of the day. This was the method at the Williamsons, so I quickly learnt how to keep my own clothes in order—and I never grew to enjoy the task.

Other homes had petrol irons, with a small tank of fuel and a pilot light to produce the heat required. Such irons were sometimes involved in accidents, but while I was at Weabonga, no one was injured from one.

All the children and men always wore clean clothes, well ironed although often patched and darned. Having learnt the effort required to achieve this, I admired all the mothers for looking after their families so well.

This was just one reason I developed a huge respect for the Weabonga women. They faced massive challenges and repetitive hard work every day of the week. Given no aids and driven by devotion to their families, each woman created a nurturing home and reared happy, healthy, respectful children. The women gave their all to ensure the best outcomes possible for the kids. I felt I had to match, if not better, their commitment.

Some homes had a kerosene refrigerator, while others made do with no more than Coolgardie safes. There was always a limit to fresh food. The men slaughtered a beast from time to time and skinned, cleaned and dressed it ready to be butchered and cut up into large pieces. The women were efficient at slicing off chops or steaks.

The women and children looked after large groups of chooks, which spent their days scratching happily around the yards or paddocks near the homes. At night, the chooks either came home from habit or were driven back to roost in pens by the children, then they were locked in against predation from foxes or dingoes; wild dogs weren't much of a problem around Weabonga, but foxes were always lurking. Chooks provided sufficient quantities of eggs as well as, rarely, the source of meals. The women, I noticed, would kill and clean the chook, plucking the feathers after placing the carcass in hot water. Getting a chook ready for the table was a time-consuming and messy process, and good layers were never sacrificed.

The vegetable garden was also managed by the children and their mothers. As these plots were the only source of fresh produce, they were tilled, weeded and tended most days. I could attest the quality of the produce achieved by some of the gardeners.

In winter, at school we kept a large pot on the glowing, red-hot top of the Broadway heater. Children brought along vegetables from the home gardens, and we chopped them into lightly salted water to make a soup. No matter the type of vegie available on the day, and the type of pasta, lentil or rice we added, our cold weather lunchtimes were always satisfying and, sometimes, adventurous.

There was a limit to what Bon could carry, and generally he only came on Fridays. So although a household could order in fresh bread once a week, otherwise they had to do their own baking. Judging by the titbits the children brought in their lunchboxes, most of the mothers were fine cooks. And after tennis on Sundays, I enjoyed their fresh sponges, fruit loaves, biscuits or scones.

All the children had chores to do when they arrived home after school, and many also had morning chores. If not done by a child, these chores would have to be done by a parent, and the parents were very busy people indeed. Through their assistance to their families, the children were learning essential lessons. I didn't want schoolwork to displace these vital chores—rather, I wanted the children to view their work as being conducted both at home and at school, and to feel their efforts were appreciated. Home and school were united to assist the children in reaching their potential, while enjoying their childhood.

From nine years of age, as soon as they were able, the boys ran lines of rabbit traps. Before twilight they would place out six or more traps in locations they had previously scouted. The boys were clever in identifying paths where rabbits were likely to run. They would dig in a metal trap, place paper on the steel plate in the centre, set the trap by pinning back the serrated jaws, and cover the trap with a light dusting of soil to disguise its presence and to remove any human scent. To set a trap wasn't easy, and could be dangerous if it sprang shut unexpectedly while being handled. The boys set their run of traps each Friday and Saturday in the late afternoon. Early the next morning, sometimes in frost or snow, they would walk their trap line to find what had been caught: often a rabbit or two. The boys would bring them home to clean, skin and dress. The rabbit meat was welcome to expand the family food supplies and, after being dried out on a wire frame, the skins could be sold to the hide merchant who came to the village once a month or so.

No one viewed trapping as other than cruel but it had to be done. The money was saved by the boys for their trips to town, which were infrequent in most families. From their earliest years the boys contributed significantly to their family through their rabbiting along with their regular chores.

It seemed to me the girls contributed equally to the boys but in ways considered appropriately feminine. All the girls were gaining skills in cooking, and the older girls would often refer to the dinner they'd prepared for the whole family one night on a weekend. All described collecting fruits in season, and the processes they employed to bottle and preserve the harvest or to transform it into jams and conserves. Additionally, the girls were learning to knit, to sew, to dress-make, to darn—in fact, to be 'good' housewives. Each girl shadowed her mother at home, engaging with her in the tasks of women in country households.

The boys, who shadowed their dads, liked nothing better than to accompany their father on a day while he was working outdoors. This was one way the boys could spend increased time with their dads, and not only did they observe the tasks and processes with which their fathers engaged—life lessons in themselves—but often they would assist in significant ways. Fencing with an offsider was always easier than fencing alone, and the same applied to rounding up the stock, collecting firewood, and even working in the shearing sheds. The boys could be genuinely useful as an additional pair of hands, as could the girls.

Sometimes as I was walking or driving away from the school in the late afternoon light, I would notice one or more of the boys tracking their dad closely around the home yard or across a roadside paddock. The long evening shadows turned both figures into giants, and each dark image merged into the other.

28

Striking moments and events accumulated as the children and I worked our way through 1961.

Our folk dancing culminated in entry into the Tamworth City Eisteddfod, in the Small Primary School Folk Dancing competition. We were represented by eight of the kids from Grades Five and Six. We had practised quite a lot, in lunchbreaks and even after school in the last week. Parents who'd been sceptical of the dancing experiment were now supportive, and the P and C arranged for the transport of all eighteen children to Tamworth for the day.

Each entrant school had to provide the music to accompany their competition dance, and ours was supplied by an LP record on the school player. Freeing me to care for the children, a parent took responsibility for carrying the player to Tamworth and getting it ready when our team's turn came to show their steps. But when the parent tried to start the music, and the kids were in position on the floor of the town hall, nothing happened. The player was broken. Catastrophe!

The judges, though, were very sympathetic. They noted the children's dismay and suggested they perform their routine without the music. Better than that, prompted a couple of kids, the non-dancers could sing the accompaniment. Bemused judges agreed.

The singing started, the dancers performed as well as they had ever trained, and the judges 'highly commended' us. To the Weabonga school community, which had never before won anything that anyone could remember, this award was better than an Olympic gold medal.

On another memorable occasion, Tom alerted all the children to his secondary science studies of the solar system.

Weabonga's night skies were so brilliant and crowded that all the children had a fascination for the stars and planets. All knew the evening and morning stars, all could find the Southern Cross, and all made guesses of the number of objects sparkling above them. Back in April, everyone in Weabonga had scanned the night sky in an effort to spy Yuri Gagarin circling above us as the first human in space.

With the children's imaginations piqued by Tom's reports, their conversations about the night skies carried on for weeks, even after he'd completed his set of correspondence school lessons.

It was Jack who suggested, 'Could we make a solar system in our schoolroom?'

Enthusiasm rocketed around the group. The project also appealed mightily to me, as I could see the opportunity for planning and cooperation, for creative activities in reading, maths, craft and art, and possibilities for all the children to make a relevant contribution.

We had limited access to basic information, as we had for all activities in that little room. But Tom's correspondence school lesson material had some detail, and we had an old set of Arthur Mee's *Children's Encyclopaedia*—from about 1937, so I hoped the information was still correct. The children quizzed their parents, who delivered further facts. It was sufficient for a basic project.

Everyone brought in old newspapers, which we set to soak in some tubs to deteriorate into papier-mâché. Children collected wires of all gauges, from thick fencing wire to that used for picture hanging and fishing. Scraps of chicken wire were brought along too.

We then agreed on the questions we must answer.

'In what galaxy is our planet Earth?'

'What is our solar system?

'What is a planet?'

'How many planets in our system?'

'What is the size of each planet?'

That question prompted, 'How are we to show each planet in our room? How can we make them a correct size? Some are big and others are small, so what will we do about building them to the right size?'

Tom had learnt of scaling and ratios, so he was very helpful. The four older kids, now in Grade Six, cottoned on quickly to the need for a way to reference Earth against the other planets and build them to a scale that fitted in our space. The three older girls, working together, took on the task of measuring and cutting the fencing wire that would form the grid upon which to layer the chicken wire as the base for plastering on the mulchy paper. To get this right, the girls had to understand the concepts of radius and circumference, and to work out the relative lengths of wire they must cut.

The girls explained to the boys, 'We are used to measuring because we help our mums do dressmaking from patterns. We know about making sure we're accurate.'

The smaller children were asked to identify the colours for each planet and to take on the work of painting them once the paper had dried.

Jack came up with a method for attaching the relevant moons and satellites through using medium-gauge wire. Lindie suggested how to attach cellophane circles for the rings of Saturn. Vickie led Carol and Susie in cutting out silver stars to form the Milky Way over the ceiling.

Within a week we had our own planetarium. Dangling from the ceiling were globes representing each planet, all pretty correct in size, placement and colour. Earth's moon had been meticulously constructed to show its mountain ranges, seas and craters, and Debbie had etched some scientific names upon this surface in tiny neat letters; we couldn't actually read them but all knew they were there.

In the corner furthest from the entry, the older boys had created an arc of the sun, in correct relative size to Earth.

Parents came along to marvel at this feat and commend the children. Bon dropped in as he'd heard about our plans and contributed some silver paper. Visitors remarked that families had taken to searching the night sky for the planets. Those with binoculars had passed them around so all the kids got a chance to look more closely at the universe in which our tiny village and tiny, tiny school found their home. June said to me, 'It was strange. Here we all were as a family lying on our backs at night out in the paddock. We all talked about the remoteness and isolation we were looking at in the night sky—such great distances. But doing that as a family brought us closer together.'

29

I learnt that when World War II came, Weabonga families, already living in conditions of some privation, had additional worries. All were concerned that the men might have to go off to fight. Reports that living conditions actually became a little easier, though, surprised me—as more nations joined the war, prices for farm produce began to increase. The Weabonga parents explained things to me.

'Well, armies and soldiers everywhere. Everyone needed uniforms, didn't they? Everyone needed wool. Everyone needed bully beef. Prices went up and the farms began to pay again.'

'And country men from around here began to sign up. So any work became shared by the fewer able men left around about.'

Max told me, 'Our dad was too old to go so he got steadier work and the family had more money. Things were still tough but we could always have a proper feed.'

Later the war extended to the Pacific, and further changes came. I was shocked by some of what I heard happened then.

'We kind'a loved the Japs,' Bill claimed.

'What? You actually loved the Japanese?' I had to ask.

'Yeah, mate. As soon as the yellow peril started their war in the Pacific, things improved for us.'

Incredulous, I said, 'Tell me more.'

So Bill went on. 'Prices for rural stuff continued to get better. Our dads got even more work. Things improved for us all.'

'Mum began to put on some pounds. She got a bit roly-poly. Bit pudgy. Different Mum.'

'Sure thing. We were all a little bit happier.'

No one denied, though, that although living had improved, they all felt in danger.

Monica told of the worries of the time. 'Everyone was talking about a possible invasion. And everyone was talking of the atrocities of the Japs in all the countries they'd invaded. Rape, torture, the killing of women, children and babies. Starvation. All that stuff.'

The parents told me that everyone knew Java and Timor had fallen to the Japanese Army. Although the government tried to hide the bombings of Darwin and Broome from the public, these events quickly became known even in a place as remote as Weabonga. All felt an invasion was just a matter of time.

Max said, 'As kids we'd play at killing the Nips. And we were prepared to do it. We were too young to join up. But we weren't too young to get ready for an invasion.'

Between Max, Bill, Tony and Vic, I heard much about this.

'We knew the bush. We'd wandered the country around here since we were kids. We'd camped out, become hunters, we could shoot and trap, we got to fish and catch yabbies in all the back-country creeks. We knew the bush and were ready to fight for it even as youngsters.'

'Yeah, mate. The bush could be our shelter. We could work with it. But the bush can be dangerous—it can work against you if you don't know it. We would have made sure the Japs were slaughtered if they followed us into the bush.'

Through these discussions I learnt a lot about the surrounding country.

I was told, 'All the farms back on to Crown land. All empty and wild. No tracks or roads into a lot of it. No fire trails. Nothing.'

'On the western side, behind the Williamson, Moran and McCrae properties, there's just wild country until you get almost to Dungowan, about fifteen miles as the bird flies.'

'We all used to climb the Sugarloaf. She's south of the village. You see her as you take the Weabonga turn-off.'

The men pointed in the direction of the mountain.

'Well, she's well over three thousand feet. Bloomin' rocky country, bushy, and with huge darn trees and thick scrub. Hard to move through. No Jap could follow us or beat us there.'

All the village men, as boys and lads, knew the back country. They'd spent weekends and holiday periods exploring and enjoying the wilderness. They said they loved the bush as much as they loved their own homes. And they loved their homes and their families, so they wouldn't stand by and watch while the 'little yellow bastards', their enemy, came to destroy them. They said they would have been prepared to kill invaders. These Weabonga men, even as lads, were used to slaughtering stock for their meat and shooting feral animals and wildlife—to kill a person wouldn't be easy for any of them but, if necessary, they probably would.

'If it was us or them, mate, what would you do?'

As lads they'd concocted a plan to escape into the bush together to engage in a running war with ambush and fast escape overland on horseback or on foot, as soon as any invader got anywhere near Weabonga. They thought their parents probably knew of their plans but turned a blind eye to them. Their mums and dads were being realistic as well.

What a feeling of horror I had that as boys and young lads, these men had needed to think about and come to terms with fighting and killing other men and, perhaps, being killed themselves.

∼

While I'd been at teachers' college, at the age of eighteen—just a little older than the Weabonga men had been, as younger teenagers, during World War II—I'd done my six months' military training in the National Service.

My then 18th Battalion, in camp at Bardia Barracks outside Ingleburn near Sydney, was encouraged to see the enemy we were preparing to kill as 'slanty-eyed commie bastards', targets for our pretend rage. I knew Australia had a long-term fear of invasion by people from Asia, but our trainers acted as though the Asian invaders were on our shore and resistance would be needed in just a matter of time. The description of our probable enemy, given by our NCO Trainers—all Korean War veterans and all pretty dysfunctional men—was always of 'slope-head, yellow bastards'.

In fact, we conscripts were browned off about the whole experience, and our enemy was more likely the army itself, which kept us in thrall.

In our barracks at night we talked quietly, trying to disentangle the puzzle in which we were trapped. What we worked out wasn't a pretty picture.

My platoon mates, mostly students at the University of Sydney, treated the National Service experience as a joke, and we all resented deeply what we saw as this complete waste of time. In our minds, it was a totally unjustifiable interruption to our lives. Much of the government reasoning behind our conscription as eighteen-year-olds we believed to be either fictitious or without serious grounds. None of us had any fear of an imminent invasion in 1957 or 1958, so we thought it was all made-up. All play-acting.

Behind our being expelled from normal society into military camps, locked up behind wire fences, our impression of society was one with a general fear of young men: greater, we believed, than any fear of an Asian communist invasion of Australia. We believed our society wanted young men to be tamed and brought to heel. We convinced each other that fear of youth, fear of us, was quite widespread, as could be seen reflected in popular films and novels: *The Wild One*, *Lord of the Flies*, *Blackboard Jungle* (which we'd all seen a few times), and the appealing films with James Dean, *Rebel Without a Cause* and *East of Eden*. Most of us had seen *Rock Around the Clock* many times in 1956 and had danced ourselves ragged in the St James Theatre. We'd no doubt that youth frightened adults.

So, to us, National Service was a desperate method for controlling young men. None of us believed army service would make us better citizens, as was often claimed by politicians. We saw it all as a game loaded against us, with young people having too poor a hand, and no vote, so no chance to win against strong political forces. Besides, we believed that any imminent invasion would have young guys like us enlisting voluntarily by the truckload. No need for pretend military training: we'd have been there if required.

As well, the call-up for service, supposed to apply to all eighteen-year-olds, missed so many. It was a deeply flawed strategy and deeply unequal. At night, in our gossip and musings, we convinced each other that, of course, we should have realised the government didn't have the resources to take all the nation's eighteen-year-olds into the military. The costs would have been prohibitive. Neither did the military have the capacity: their resources would have been overwhelmed. As it was, even with the limited numbers in the nation's camps, the military found itself doing little other than inadequately training teenage conscripts. We supposed the government had to find a way to limit intake numbers without appearing to do so.

Out of eighteen regular players of my Rugby League team at the local Kensington Church Youth Group, I was the only one conscripted. All the others had flat feet. From the Balmain Teachers' College group of my peers, comprising about fifty physically able young men, I remember only three of us being called up. Yet these trainee teachers had all been passed medically and physically fit to take up a college scholarship. In the barracks, we surmised medical testing was being used to contain numbers. That the majority of eighteen-year-old Australian males failed the intake medical test was an indictment on the nation—if it reflected reality, then our generation was so unwell and so desperately unfit. We didn't believe the medical problems were real, so those of us forced into the training voiced our bitter resentment. Political make-believe; political claptrap.

In Weabonga, I heard there was nothing new in that. As I matured I was becoming less surprised by political chicanery, so I readily accepted the corresponding view being conveyed by the Weabonga parents of their experience in the 1940s. I heard from them of deliberate government obfuscation and outright lying during the war. The parents spoke about government plans to abandon much of Australia if an invasion occurred—a plan totally denied by the government at the time but widely discussed.

The Weabonga men were giving me facts. Their intention to take to the bush hadn't been a joke. For them, back then, this was real: the enemy was almost on the Australian shore.

A couple of the local men, including Lawrie, had joined up. Lawrie never spoke of it, but neither did the other ex-servicemen. Others, too young then to enlist, had lots to say, though. They'd taken on the message of scorched earth. All understood, as thirteen- to sixteen-year-olds, there was a government plan to abandon much of the country to the invaders, to the enemy. The men claimed, 'We were going to become guerrilla fighters. We were good shots. We were going to hit and run, kill and disappear. We could have beaten them.'

Monica had grown up in the area, but the other women had married into Weabonga families. They backed their husbands, though.

'If we'd had been teenagers in Weabonga during the war, there'd have been ways we could support the boys who'd taken to the bush. I think we'd have been game enough to help them.'

'We'd have done food drops, message drops. Gosh, we'd have sabotaged Japanese equipment if we'd had a chance.'

Such stories told me that, through necessity, the Weabonga lads and girls had needed to become self-reliant, committed and loyal, determined and ready to accept the hardest of realities and work creatively together to overcome difficulties. They had carried all the positive outcomes with them into parenthood.

I asked the parents how their own growing up and the way they'd been parented were affecting the way they were raising their own kids.

'Greatly,' they all admitted.

'We did pretty well, even in difficult times. The way we were brought up helped us. We reckon our mum and dad did right by us. Why would we change? We want our kids to learn the lessons we learnt. We want our kids to be good, hardworking and truthful, just as our parents wanted us to be. Don't you think that's right, Pete?'

'Mate, the only difference,' I would hear, 'is we want our kids to be happy and free from worry. Of course our own parents wanted that for us. But, gee whiz, life is a hell of a lot easier now than when we were growing up. No need for our kids to miss out.'

In many significant ways, though, the life of the present-day village children was, I thought, at its core not that different to the life led by their own mums and dads twenty years or more before, in the 1930s and '40s.

Actually, the lives of the 1960s village children weren't that far removed from agrarian life in medieval times. Sometimes, on a hot day in summer of our final term together, as we worked through the morning, I found myself daydreaming that an Angelus bell might ring out at noon over the village from the Catholic chapel. A teaching monk from the Middle Ages would, I daydreamed, feel right at home in our company.

30

Patricia and I discussed spending our lives together, and towards the end of term two in 1961 we got engaged. Maybe it was the case, as Patricia later claimed, that the only way for her to stop my awful Saturday morning caterwauling over the phone was to agree to marry me. I don't believe so—she was just joshing, surely?

Patricia decided to return to Sydney and we planned to be married in the next year. I was over the moon and, eager to have her nearer me, arranged to drive to Melbourne in the September school holidays to collect and bring her back north.

My little car beetled down the New England Highway and set out onto the Hume. I sang all the way in anticipation and happiness. With no one to overhear, I just let my emotions gush out, and they distracted me enough that a long drive seemed but a small hiccup. Probably every Everly Brothers song, all the Elvis love ballads, some Frankie Laine, Billy Daniels and Little Richard got an airing—anything with a message about love, and a solid beat. The songs reeled up the miles, bringing me nearer to my desire, so I didn't resent the time taken; every minute and every mile post were closing the gap.

My plan for the twelve-hour return journey to Sydney was to take time, not to rush, to relish being together, to milk the opportunity to talk about our future, to make plans, to cement the pact we had made. With no other company in the car we'd be able to converse openly, sharing our most honest and intimate thoughts. How I looked forward to that chance.

As part of her preparation for my visit, Patricia had visited the Randall Worth Salon for a fashionable hairdo. At that time, Randall was the hairdresser of preference for women from Melbourne's worlds of high society and entertainment. Through her role at Channel 7, Patricia had befriended him, so he was determined to do his best for her coiffure. It had been arranged that I would call in to the salon when I arrived in Melbourne to meet up with Patricia and, perhaps, commence a reunion night celebration.

So, I found the salon and called to the reception desk. After a few minutes, Patricia emerged. She looked . . . stunning.

How can I describe what I witnessed? Randall had created a spectacular vision and, accompanying her, he beamed with pleasure both at his creation and at me. We shook hands. I was knocked for six, without the ability to respond appropriately. Unable to express my pleasure at meeting my friend or my appreciation of Randall's art, I simply stood transfixed, mouth wide open, gasping. I knew I was being unmannerly but, it was true, I couldn't help myself.

Sometimes fashions just can't be explained and seem to have no sensible genesis. And, in their turn, fashions go and, perhaps years or decades later, return. The styling of Patricia's hair that afternoon was a fashion that came, went fairly quickly and has never returned. As a wonderful treat, Randall had teased, trained, trellised, transfixed and transfigured her hair into, it seemed, the world's highest and widest beehive.

Somehow the hair was standing, in the most amazing bouffant confection, as an almost circular tower that reached perhaps a foot above her head. The whole thing seemed rigid, with no chance of unravelling: it appeared to have been set with cement. Not one hair escaped the cairn.

The description of such styling as a beehive is most apt. It did have the appearance of an old-style conical English beehive, woven from straw, as seen in illustrations of nineteenth-century novels. Why on earth, I wondered, did my friend have such a thing perching atop her head?

Later she explained that the hair was able to defy gravity and stay in place only by the application of cans of hairspray, and she also explained that, as the only way to rid the hair of this spray-on goo was to shampoo it away, many young women maintained the expensive styling for months at a time. Rumours abounded of nests of beetles and even mice taking up residence in some of these hair palaces.

However, that afternoon I had been struck speechless. In anticipating our reunion, I had imagined Patricia appearing in the way with which I was most familiar and which I found most endearing. I thought she was beautiful, and one of my delights was her rich, thick hair, simply cut to rest above her shoulders, framing her lovely face. Now her hair stood to attention, raising its wiry tendrils way above her head. It was unbelievable and, to me, disturbing. I should have known better and found the initiative to commend what I saw. I regretted immediately that I was unable to do so—my dumb silence was unfair to both of them. After a minute or two I regained some composure and expressed a few feeble compliments, but the damage had been done. I could see I had hurt Randall's feelings and discountenanced my friend. This wasn't the way I'd planned for our getting back together to occur. I could have kicked myself. *Silly, silly man.*

Randall disappeared from our lives when we left his salon. And, to my absolute relief, Patricia's upset didn't last long. She confessed, 'I could detect your shock when I came out of Randall's. This beehive hairdo wasn't my idea. I'd been quite overwhelmed by Randall's enthusiasm for it, so I'd just gone along with him. Once he had commenced, though, I could see what was happening, and I was quite dismayed. I couldn't find the courage to ask him to stop, though—I thought that would be too critical of his work, and I wanted to avoid any embarrassment or discomfort for him. So, against my best judgement, I let it happen. I think the hairdo ludicrous and will get rid of it as soon as possible.'

How relieved I was.

Patricia's kind, self-effacing treatment of Randall was characteristic of her. She would tolerate some situations not to her personal benefit because she could see that others were obtaining something they liked or desired. She would put herself out for people. I've always loved that about her.

It took only the morning's hair wash for the awful concoction to disappear.

⁓

I was introduced next morning to Patricia's flatmates, who explained they felt they already knew me: they'd enjoyed listening to my 'crooning' and to some censored snippets from my letters. I was initially a little taken aback. But, on reflection, I saw it was just a part of the inclusiveness and openness that had attracted me to this wonderful woman who loved sharing her joy with friends.

That morning, I was surprised to see Patricia's twelve-year-old sister, Janet, sitting on the couch. Patricia said she'd been visiting over the first week of her school holidays. Then came some unexpected news: Janet was to accompany us to Sydney.

Blood rushed to my head. This wasn't part of my plan. I wanted a private ride, just the two of us. My temper was rising, and some unkind words were close to expulsion. Instantly my inner voice shouted: *Idiot. Have you learnt nothing of worth from yesterday's hairstyle incident? Calm down! Now! Be gracious. You can do this.*

So, I said, 'How terrific. We can get to know each other so much better as future in-laws on our trip.'

There were several cases and bags to load, as Patricia had packed up almost two years of her Melbourne life to take home. Little sister had her own port. We filled the boot of my small car, and when the three of us got in, the vehicle was weighed down but not dangerously.

Off we set, and after travelling about a hundred yards I was asked to call in to an address in South Melbourne where we were to pick up a friend, John, who was taking a holiday in Sydney and was to travel with us at Patricia's invitation.

I had a feeling this wasn't going to work out well—but, having adopted a conciliatory stance, I proceeded to the given address. I was quickly resigned to yet another travelling companion.

John was waiting for us along with several suitcases of clothes that he felt necessary to keep him well presented on all possible occasions during his two weeks in Sydney. My small boot was full, so we sat his ports on the back shelf, and between him and Patricia's sister on the back seat. With the four of us now in place, the car was certainly overloaded. The springs began lurching.

Off we set again. No more surprises, so we tackled the highway. All went well until somewhere past Albury.

We started to climb up a long, gradual slope. The road went on and up. No top to the hill was in sight. The little car began to labour. My eyes shot to the temperature gauge, but wishing had no impact. The car boiled over and just died. Here were the four of us, miles from anywhere, with my biscuit tin not willing to carry its load any further.

After a whole lot of difficult, time-consuming and vexatious arrangements, and a night in an Albury hotel, the next day we got back on the road. Carrying an emergency can of water, which from time to time we decanted into the radiator, we achieved a slow, although not unhappy progress to our home town.

Having John with us through these troubles turned out to be a joy. He was a bright, witty conversationalist. Coming from a background of creating and directing shows for metropolitan TV stations, he had loads of inside stories and many funny anecdotes about the celebrities of the day. We shared much fun and laughter.

John was an educated chap. He loved poetry and, with a captive audience, could easily be encouraged to recite his favourites. Hopkins and Wilde received John's full, emotive treatment, with his enthralling version of 'The Windhover', and his full-length, compelling telling of the 'Ballad of Reading Gaol'. His favourite, quite obscure stories from English history also distracted our attention and kept us relatively content.

Poetry was already a link between Patricia and me. She knew many Shakespeare sonnets off by heart and recited those for us. Her rendition of Sonnet 18, 'Shall I Compare Thee to a Summer's Day?', had me doing just that with regard to her as we sat patiently waiting by the roadside. All of us took part in remembering bits of *Twelfth Night*, *Hamlet*, the 'Scottish Play' and others. I contributed several poems, including 'South of My Days', and explained how Judith Wright's words had crystallised much about Weabonga for me.

Through that journey, John and I became firm friends, and he remained a central and important part of our lives.

Courting is a process. The Hume Highway epic journey added to my understanding of the character, style and attitudes of Patricia. She was a very social person, making strong friends whom she came to adore and to whom she was immensely loyal. If I was to share life with her I must agree to—indeed, welcome—others sharing our life. And that encouraged me. Life was ours to make as we wished. If having many loving friends was central to Patricia, it was central to me.

Before we might begin building our future together, though, I had one more term to complete in Weabonga. Patricia and I would be separated for another three months, but I could face this with equanimity and composure, knowing our plans.

At Weabonga I would ensure the kids and I achieved as much together as possible. My desire was for them all to be capable of success no matter what was to follow.

31

During the final term I invited two local men to talk to the older children about the district's history. Tom and Jack, among others, had begun to ask questions that I couldn't answer with my limited classroom resources. My casual chats with Allan Watermain and Tim Bourke had shown me that both possessed a store of relevant knowledge.

The men were hesitant about my invite. 'I'm not used to talking with children,' Allan explained—but, with a little urging, he agreed.

All the children were acquainted with Tim, as he'd been the postmaster. Allan's face they recognised although they didn't know him well.

Allan volunteered to lead the way. He came in one Tuesday after lunch, and the children settled well, eager for him to commence. Remembering how shy they'd been when I first came, and how silent they had been during Mr Flood's inspections,

I was encouraged to see the relative ease they adopted for this talk.

On behalf of the students, Lindie thanked the visitor and welcomed him to the schoolroom. All Fours, Fives and Sixes, along with Tom, gathered around near the blackboard. A large map of New South Wales was ready.

The first question came from Tom and, given his interest in eventually becoming a landowner, wasn't unexpected. 'How did the country around here get taken up for sheep farming?'

Allan, a descendant of one of the colony's most famous and important explorers, was the perfect source for sensible answers about sheep grazing.

First, he asked, 'Do you know of squatters?'

Tom said, 'I think they were early settlers who just came and took whatever land they wanted.'

'Pretty right,' said Allan. 'That is the way land was settled by whites in this district. Sheep men just arrived, saw what they liked, so took possession. They had no legal right to it.'

'When did the white men arrive here?' queried Jack.

Pointing to Bathurst on the map, while running his finger along to point out paths taken, Allan answered. 'John Oxley was the first white man to come through here. In 1818 he made an exploration trip starting in Bathurst.' Allan pointed. 'Oxley explored to the west to begin, mapping the Macquarie River for a way, but then turned east hoping to find a route back down to the coast.' The children easily followed Allan's finger. 'Oxley was a surveyor. So he was expert in making the first large maps of places he explored. He made a map of his trip, and we can still see his map today. There are no records of any earlier white people in this area before Oxley's 1818 trip.'

Joe murmured, 'The bush would have been terrible thick back then. How long a time did he explore?'

'Oh, you're right,' Allan agreed. 'He travelled through the bush for many months. Looking at his map for his trip he must have walked near here to the north when he was heading to the coast.' Allan pointed out a path crossing the Moonbi Range to the north of Tamworth and travelling in the direction of Walcha.

'What did he find?' many children asked at once.

'Well, in his journal he wrote that the area up here in the high country was lovely. Grassy with trees spread about. He described it as just like a park. Do you know how a park looks? Lots of lawn areas and trees here and there? Just like your schoolyard, really.'

'Oh, yair. Just like the picnic area near the Chaffey Dam,' said Lindie.

'Exactly. Trees around, just as spread out as that.' Allan continued, 'When Oxley reported what he'd seen, he caught the interest of men who were looking for new places to run sheep and start a sheep station. They liked his description of the lovely grass and wide areas to run stock, so they began to drive sheep up into the area from down around Newcastle and Maitland. The first settled sheep run we know of anywhere near here was called Wolka, settled in 1832.' Allan wrote the name on the board—W, o, l, k, a—and asked, 'Does that remind you of something?'

'Yes,' called out Lindie. 'That's just a different spelling for w, a, l, c, h, a. That's where the town of Walcha is now.'

'Well done,' Allan encouraged.

Will followed up with, 'But who was the first person to run sheep around here at Weabonga?'

'We know it was a man named Peter Brodie. In 1841 Peter squatted on land near what is Limbri today. Remember, a squatter is a person who just takes over land that they want, and that's exactly what Brodie did.'

'Was he the only one?' called out Rick.

Allan explained, 'Brodie squatted deliberately at Limbri because it's the entrance to the valley of the Swamp Oak Creek. By setting up there, Brodie stopped anyone else passing him by to take land further up the valley. Do you understand how he could keep other squatters out by doing that?'

'Was it because no one would be able to drive their sheep around him?' Tom asked. 'It wouldn't be easy to push a mob of sheep over the steep hills to get past.'

'Good answer. What Brodie did was to settle what they call a "keyhole station". Do you know a keyhole?'

Vickie, bravely for her, spoke up. 'We have keyholes on our doors. I think Mum has keys somewhere but they're never in the locks. A key in the lock can keep the door closed.'

Jimmy, who in Grade Two wasn't supposed to be in the group listening to Allan, piped up. 'None of our doors are ever locked though, so we don't need the keys.' I loved Jimmy's unflagging desire to know about everything, so I wasn't about to dissuade him.

'Yes,' Allan said, 'keys in keyholes can lock things away. That's what Brodie was able to do—lock up the valley from Limbri to well above here, up nearly to Ingelba, all to himself.' Allan looked around but the children were keeping up. 'His property stopped anyone else from squatting anywhere above him in the valley. Beside his main home at Limbri he had another near here. That home must have been right near your schoolyard. The area here, around that hut, was called Rywung. I'm sure you know that the name Rywung was changed to Weabonga.'

'Swamp Oak, Rywung, Weabonga,' offered Will.

'Right,' said Allan. 'The furthest point of Brodie's run was right up the top of the creek near the next squatter's station, Bungendore, above where Ingelba is today. You know Ingelba, don't you?'

'Golly, that's a long, long way, isn't it?' Lindie suggested. She knew because her home farm was on the way to Ingelba. 'I suppose he must have been able to run lots of sheep?'

'Yes, he certainly was. His stock return of the late 1880s showed he had fifty-two thousand acres and was shearing twenty-two thousand sheep—a huge station.'

Tom was keenly interested in all Allan had to say and asked, 'How did he look after so many sheep spread so widely apart?'

Allan said, 'Brodie couldn't put up fences. There was no fencing wire when he was setting up. So what do you think he did to care for that number of sheep on such a large property?'

The children thought in silence for a while.

Tom suggested, 'The sheep would have needed looking after. There would have been dingoes back then.' Another long pause, and Tom added, 'He might have had people looking after the sheep.'

'That's exactly right, Tom. Brodie had shepherds. There were shepherd's huts every few miles, including the one here at Rywung near our school and near Bungendore further up the creek.'

On the blackboard Allan drew a rough map of the Swamp Oak Creek between Ingelba and Limbri. He then made some marks on the map and pointed to places. 'Brodie would have had shepherd's huts about where today's homesteads and properties are along the creek down to Limbri today. So there would have been maybe twenty shepherd's huts along the creek, with one of them near about where my own property is.' Then he pointed again to the board: 'Where the Williamsons are,' he said, and pointed again, 'and here where you live, Joe.'

Joe nodded. 'Yeah, my dad told me something about that.'

Allan described how the shepherds had been single men, a mixture of convicts, ticket-of-leave men, ex-convicts and a few free settlers. None stayed long—the life of a shepherd was isolated, lonely and at times dangerous, Allan explained.

'No sheep station around here now is anywhere as big as Brodie's place,' Debbie suggested. 'How did smaller farms happen then?'

Allan replied, 'Well, Brodie only had a licence to use the land. It still belonged to the government. Laws were brought in that made it easy for people to lay claim to land if they had settled it for a while. The government wanted to break up the huge landholdings of the first squatters and encouraged other people to settle on smaller areas.'

The newer laws encouraged numbers of small settlers, and Brodie couldn't stop them.

Later, in the late 1880s, gold had begun to be mined around Rywung, and Allan told the children that its discovery brought many changes apart from the mining. 'By the late 1880s there were several hundred miners around the Rywung area, and they began to settle small areas and run some stock for food. Settlement meant they could apply for that portion and so they took over land as well.' Allan then asked, 'I wonder what you might know about the goldmining?'

'My dad told me there were terribly many people,' Will called out. 'He said about five hundred miners and people in Rywung.'

'Your dad would certainly know,' responded Allan. 'Your Grandad Baulderstone was one of the miners here in the 1890s, wasn't he?'

'Yair, and so was the Williamsons' grandpa,' acknowledged Will. 'My dad said Richard Williamson was one of the men who owned the Highland Mary mine.'

Allan continued on for maybe another twenty minutes that afternoon: goldmines, miners, shops, hotels, pubs, crushers, yields, Highland Mary, Rising Moon, Storm King. And the children maintained their concentration until near the end.

Tom could have chatted with Allan for much longer. Allan must have detected the interest and spontaneously invited the young man to meet up with him at the Sunday tennis where they could extend their discussion. Tom accepted. I was surprised by both the offer and the agreement, as neither of them had ever been to the tennis as far as I knew. It looked like a good friendship for Tom was in the making.

Over the following days, the kids wrote their versions of a new story, 'The Settlement of Weabonga'. They developed a booklet to contain all the information, along with hand-drawn maps and illustrations. Allan's visit had been a great success, of which all the families had a full recount, and parents made favourable comments about his inclusion in the school lessons.

⌒

Following on from Allan's visit, and its emphasis on farming and mining, the children asked me about Indigenous people in the area. Jack was particularly curious, asking, 'Were there black people here before Mr Brodie came with all his sheep?'

I wondered about the level of Jack's understanding of his own inheritance. Was he deliberately seeking deeper knowledge about this?

We had no resources in the school to answer Jack's question, and I was a poor witness to the precolonial history of the region. In order to close the knowledge gap, I suggested to Jack that we ask his grandfather, Tim, who had already agreed to talk with the children. I assured Jack that during my afternoon chats with Tim, having a drink together on the post office veranda, I'd heard much relevant information, so his grandfather would be able to answer lots of questions. Jack approved.

So Tim's planned visit was timely, and a week later he attended. He had confided to me that Allan had been 'skiting' of his successful time at the school and of how much he'd enjoyed himself with the kids. Tim had found this encouraging and felt himself more ready to talk to the young audience.

Prompted by Tim, and knowing about the intention of his talk, I'd prepared a rough blackboard map of the local area.

That afternoon, Tim was welcomed to the school by Debbie and thanked for his attendance by Mike. The old postmaster immediately explained he was a little nervous and asked that the students hold their questions. He said, 'I'm not used to talking to groups of people. I'll settle down as I get some confidence. Just hold on and ask me your questions a little later.'

All the children nodded.

Off Tim went, in a bit of a rush. 'Mr Watermain told you that the first white man in our area was John Oxley. Oxley's journal contained descriptions of grassy, park-like areas with scattered trees. Perfect, he thought, for sheep. Well, I'll tell you how and why the place looked like a park.' Tim paused, a little dramatically. He was beginning to enjoy himself. 'Fire! Yes, through fire! Deliberate use of fire!'

'Oxley wrote that black people were seen—"natives", he named them—but they walked away and avoided Oxley so that his men couldn't talk with them. Oxley learnt nothing from the local blacks. But he knew from elsewhere that Aborigines used fire to prepare a good place for hunting. New grass shoots spring up after fire, and kangaroos, wallabies and other animals come to eat them. Fire also kept country lightly covered with trees.'

It was about here that Tim made his first real stop, perhaps to gather his breath, and I made discreet hand signals to suggest he slow down—always a schoolteacher.

Jack used the break to ask his grandfather, 'Did Oxley see the black men hunting? Did they have boomerangs?'

Tim, having recovered, went on at an easier pace. 'Well, no, Jack. Oxley didn't see any real hunting. But he saw something he'd never before seen. He found large nets hanging between trees. There were nets near the ground and some up high in the air. The nets could only have been made by the natives. Oxley and his men thought the blacks must use the nets to catch animals or birds they herded in. That was a clever way to hunt.'

Tim was clearly now more relaxed, and the children must have felt encouraged to begin questioning.

The girls wanted to know, 'How did the blacks make their nets and what did they use to make them?' Handicrafts always aroused the girls' interests.

Tim said, 'The Aborigines, we think, used grasses and rushes they teased out into long strips and then into strings to weave together to make a fine but strong net. Those spiky rush plants that grow down near the Swamp Oak Creek would do the job real well, I reckon. But, with the white men coming, bringing all their sheep, the hunting grounds that the natives used gradually were closed off to them. They moved away from near the sheep stations to live in their own, more isolated, camps.'

Tom's interest was piqued, and he queried, 'Where did they live? What did they eat?'

Tim answered, 'Mr Watermain told you about shepherds on Brodie's station, didn't he? Some Aboriginal men became shepherds for Brodie on his Swamp Oak Station and up on Bungendore Station, the other station above Ingelba—nearer to Niangala—as well. There were a few black men as miners too. When I was a boy, there were several settlements of Aborigines around about. The nearest to us was at Ingelba, not far away. There had been settlements at Walcha and Nowendoc as well. So there were quite a few Aborigines about when I was younger. They didn't die out or just disappear altogether.'

'Yes, but what did they eat?' Will repeated.

'I have to tell you that sometimes they took sheep from Brodie's flocks. That caused trouble, but the natives probably thought that if Brodie had taken their hunting grounds they could take some of his sheep. On top of that, the blacks had hunted these areas for a long time—no one knows how long, but many, many years. They knew the country well. Even today if you camp along the Macdonald River up there above Ingelba, where the blacks settled, you'll find it easy enough to catch good feeds of yabbies and a few fish, and, if you're clever, pull in a few ducks as well. The blacks were great hunters, living well off the land. It was the white man's coming with their sheep that made it hard for them.'

'Are there still some Aborigines today?' many children asked at once.

'Yes, of course. You'll remember that little boy, Steven Walls, who was lost near Guyra last year. Well a black tracker helped to find him. That man was Jim Boney. There are still Boneys living around Ingelba, and I think the man who found Steven might have been part of that family.'

Tim went on, 'Here's a good tale. Mr Watermain talked to you last week about the three names for our village—Swamp Oak, Rywung and Weabonga. Where do you think those names come from? That's right; apart from Swamp Oak, the other two are Aboriginal names. Now here's how we know them.'

This had the children agog.

'Perc Buckland, whom you all know—lives over on that hill over there? Well, Perc, who's lived here a lot longer than me, told me once that the post office wanted to change the name from Rywung in 1916, that's forty-five years ago. Perc said the post office people were upset that so much of the mail was going to the wrong Rywung. There were other Rywungs in other places as well as the Rywung here, all getting mixed up.'

'Golly, that would be a mess,' Debbie suggested.

Tim nodded. 'Anyway, Perc spoke with "King Yarrie", the king of the blacks. He lived around Nowendoc back then in 1916.'

'King Yarrie. A real king. Yarrie,' murmured Jack.

'Perc said King Yarrie told him that Ingelba meant "the place of the whirlpool" and Niangala meant "the place of the eclipse". Perc said that King Yarrie had given that name to Niangala himself because he was there when an actual eclipse occurred.'

In our work on the solar system we had discussed eclipses, so the children knew what Tim meant. I hadn't known the translation of Niangala but was pleased that our various school activities were dovetailing so well.

'What about our village name?' Lindie called out.

'Rywung was "the meeting place or resting place". Perc told the post office that as Rywung's meaning reflected the place so well, the local people wanted to keep Rywung as the village name. The post office just changed the name to Weabonga, and nobody was happy. Weabonga means "swamp gum", pretty much the same as swamp oak, so the post office must have thought it should continue with that close meaning.'

(When I heard Tim's explanation I set to wondering if I had misheard Bon and his telling me about the Weabonga name on my first day almost two years back. I really liked it when Bon said that Weabonga meant 'the meeting place between the hills', so I thought I'd just stick, in my mind, with what I'd believed for two years.)

'Who was Yarrie the king of?' Joe quickly put in.

Tim hesitated a little before answering. 'A bit hard to know, and I'm not certain. There were quite a number of tribes among the blacks. They didn't all come from the one tribe. From what people have told me over the years, the nearest blacks to here came probably from a tribe called the Himberong. They were most likely the people who lived near Ingelba. There may be Himberong descendants still living around up there even today.'

The children chattered excitedly. There was a lot for them to take in, so Tim didn't go on for much longer.

As the kids settled in to nut out how they would write about Tim's story, I walked with him towards the school gate. 'Tim, how the children enjoyed this afternoon with you, thanks so much,' I said. 'I kept my eye on Jack particularly. He was taking it in avidly. I do hope he really enjoyed it.'

'I noticed that response from Jack as well. I'm sure we've got many new openings for talking about matters. That's good!' And then Tim said, 'I didn't tell the children everything.' He paused, then went on, 'I would never tell the children about the possible massacre I've heard of.'

Shocked, I asked, 'Massacre, Tim? What are you talking about?'

'I've heard that in the late 1880s some white men used dynamite to attack the blacks' Ingelba camp.'

'My God, Tim. My God!'

'Well, I'm not too sure of the truth of it. And I'd never tell children about it even if I knew it to be true.'

'People must have been killed?'

'I believe so. There were women and children in the camp when the explosion was set off. Those who told me haven't said the exact number, but they were pretty sure there were women and children among the dead.'

Words left me. I was shaken and stunned. Until then I'd heard only the vaguest of rumours of brutality such as this. In 1961 such things were barely mentioned and were not openly discussed. A massacre had taken place literally on the doorstep of this little school. How? How could such a thing have happened?

I couldn't turn away from it: I had to double down on processing what white settlement had really meant for Indigenous Australians.

I walked slowly back to re-enter the classroom. I had to hide my shock and despair from the gaze of the children; I didn't want them to be distressed. That afternoon, as soon as I spotted that parents' cars had arrived to pick up the farm-based kids, I dismissed them earlier than our usual going-home time.

32

I needed to seek a transfer back to a Sydney school for the following year. Patricia and I were to wed and set up a home and life together. I was to enrol in a part-time degree at the University of Sydney and would return to being responsible for a single class in a single grade, giving me a chance to test how well I was now able to assist children's learning in a regular environment.

Approaching Mr Flood to discuss my plans, I explained my upcoming marriage and my desire to seek an inner-city school. Congratulating me on the wedding plans, he endorsed my decisions and revealed he was also moving to Sydney—and to an inner-city inspectorate. *Snap!* When he said he would like to help me find a teaching appointment in a school in his new inspectorate, I was really bucked up. Not only would it make the achievement of an appropriate appointment more likely, but it also gave me confidence the inspector had judged my teaching in a most positive way.

With his warm encouragement confirming my choices, I submitted my application for a transfer. I had no heavy heart in doing so. It had always been my plan to spend no more that the obligatory two years away from Sydney and, although I had enjoyed much of my experiences at Weabonga, I had no interest in extending my stay. I wanted new challenges, and I looked forward to the next important stage in my life.

My sense was that I had matured and grown considerably at Weabonga, but I was ready to move on. One challenge I had expected in becoming a teacher-in-charge in the country was that of facing isolation. At the beginning I'd wondered if I could handle the tests that being alone would bring me, as a professional, an individual and a social person. Actually, I couldn't—it was only through the rescue carried off by the Williamsons, and the unexpected emergence of Perc and Ethel as interesting companions, that I was able to settle down in Weabonga. If either of those events hadn't occurred, I would have certainly sought a transfer to a more acceptable location or resigned as a teacher.

Spending all day with kids didn't provide for me the engagement and companionship I needed to be happy and mentally healthy. Being with the children was rewarding, but it wasn't sufficient. So I'd learnt something important about my character and nature.

I felt great affection for all the children. How could I not appreciate them, having spent two years supporting their learning, growth and development? They had all changed over those two years: they were more knowledgeable, more capable, more certain both of themselves and of my positive regard for them. Daily, I experienced signs of their warm feelings for me. They were always tractable and cooperative. They were still somewhat reticent, and mostly quiet in their mannerisms and approaches, but always alert and respectful. As country kids, they were delightful, happy people, slower in their ways than city kids might have been, more circumspect about relationships with adults. They were innocent, guileless, and mainly free of negative feelings and thoughts, developing as individuals whom, I believed, would grow to be wonderful adults. As we came closer to parting, I hoped I had been truly helpful and kind to them all.

Once I was sure of my inspector's support for a transfer, I let the parents know I would be moving on.

I hadn't come to know them as well as I knew their children. With some I'd played social tennis and had a cordial, mostly superficial friendship. A few had assisted me in the P and C, so I'd come to know them better. Yarning with the village men was an occasional occurrence, and they called me their mate—I hoped that was true. I'd certainly grown to appreciate their company. However, with a few parents—such as the slightly reclusive family living in the house across the creek, or the family of our teenager and his sister—I had so little interaction that I knew almost nothing about them. This was strange, I thought, considering that in two years I'd probably spent more time with their kids than the parents had themselves.

Nearing year's end, the children and I began planning for the annual concert on the final day of the school year. We had rounded off the previous year in that way; the parents had loved it, and the children had gained enormous pleasure from being the centre of so much attention and the recipients of much praise.

The children requested, as a centrepiece and finale, the presentation of the nativity in the Bethlehem stable. They loved the central role of animals and cherished the idea of dressing up as old-time shepherds or wise kings, which the boys saw as their roles, or as angels, with all the girls happy to don little wings and appear soulful.

'Who will play Joseph?' the children asked, then immediately suggested Tom: 'Would you be Joseph?' They knew he was a natural leader and a responsible carer.

I waited for Tom's response, not quite sure if, at fifteen, he'd see himself taking part in this dress-up.

'Of course,' he said, 'I'd be happy to be Joseph. I can think of some ways to make a costume for an old-time carpenter. Perhaps I can make some sort of a beard as a disguise.'

'Who will be Mary, the mother of baby Jesus?' pondered young Susie, the daughter of the lay preacher.

The kids made various suggestions.

'Mary must look a bit older.'

'It can't be Debbie, though, as she's Tom's sister.'

'Needs someone quiet and respectful, who can kneel still for a long while on stage.' That was Joe. He'd grown up a lot, and his judgements were becoming reliable and no longer aimed just at raising a laugh.

'I think it should be Vickie,' Jack contributed. 'She'd be just right.'

'Vickie,' many asked, 'do you want to? You'd be real bonzer at it.'

Vickie looked taken aback. She hadn't expected this and would never have put herself forward, so she blushed and hid a little behind her hand. 'Do you really want me?' she whispered, so very quietly.

'Yes, yes. Too right we do.'

The children had worked out a scheme for basing the nativity on the Christmas carols they'd been practising. The scene would open with just Mary and Joseph in a stable, looking down on a crib in which Carol's baby doll would be tucked. Then, as the carols introduced them, the shepherds, kings and angels would enter and surround the Christ child, until the traditional tableau was complete.

Each child chose their role and inveigled their mums and dads into creating costumes. Nothing was too fancy—just the usual bath and tea towels for the shepherds. All helped to create sets of angel wings from fencing and chicken wire with strips of torn newspaper for the feathers. Crowns for the wise men came into being from cardboard and gold and silver foil, collected over weeks from cigarette packets or from the very occasional chocolate bars. For our planetarium Bon had brought us a stock of silver foil rescued from the wrapping of the power wiring the technicians used at the PO depot. And some of those silver stars could be reused on the stage set.

Tom created a baby's cradle from half a painted oil drum, mounted on wooden pieces nailed together, draped with an opened hessian sugar bag and stuffed with hay.

Nearing the afternoon of the concert, Rick suddenly called out, 'I'm goin' ta bring one of our new lambs to be on the stage.'

'Whacko,' cried Gary, 'we've some new lambs too. I'll ask Dad if we can bring one of those.'

Both families must have bred successfully from the ewes they ran on the common.

On the concert afternoon, in the hall swept and dusted by some of the mums and dads, the audience included all the parents. Also present were Tim, Perc and Ethel, Allan and Claudine Watermain, Barry White, the Williamsons, and Bon, who'd completed his mail run early so he could be there.

The audience loved the choir, the younger children's songs, the older children's choral verse speaking, the two plays, and the folk dances. As the nativity scene commenced, the adults joined in with the children's carols as they had done the year before. The arrival on stage of three lambs was watched, though, with some trepidation. The small black pellets the lambs began to deposit as their contribution received little comment, although some subdued chuckles could be heard—perhaps, all might agree, sheep dung added a touch of authenticity. But nothing was permitted to break the spell cast by the children's perform-ances, and the audience looked on with broad smiles.

The children received a standing ovation and a vote of thanks from Vic, as chair of the P and C. He presented me with an engraved silver tray expressing the community's best wishes for my upcoming wedding and their thanks for all that I had contributed to Weabonga. The presentation took me by surprise and moved me. I returned Vic's words with my own thanks for the cooperation and support they had shown both to me as the teacher and to the school. As I was a little confounded by their kindness, my response was a bit stumbling, but my words were well meant and honest and, I hoped, meaningful.

The parents accepted my speech as it was intended. They cheered and clapped, and several of the men sang out, 'Well done.'

In two years the parents had expressed nothing but acceptance of what I was attempting in their school. Never had there been anything but expressions of thanks for the efforts I'd made to help their kids. That was enough; I didn't need invitations to meals or chatty interactions with them all. They had difficult, busy lives, and they had entrusted their children to my care and supported my decisions.

As I said goodbye to the kids, many clinging to my arms, still in costume, the atmosphere was emotional. The older girls were teary, and I came close to tears as well. I hugged each child. How pleased I was that I could, with the parents present, display genuine sorrow and embrace each of the young people with whom my life had been so intertwined. We had shared our steady gains, our happy times, some exhilarating triumphs and warm camaraderie. That afternoon was the only time I hugged any of the children, and it was just, right and natural.

Leave-taking from the parents was a little easier. Their natural reticence ensured there were no tears, but I was bolstered by the steady flow of gratitude and their sincere hopes for my future happiness.

At home that night, Paul, George and I had our last meal together. The evening before, I had prepared a dinner I could quickly reheat when I returned home late after the concert.

We reminisced, picking out highlights of our time together. I made my final thanks, unable to express sufficiently my deep-felt appreciation for their generosity and support. What a marvellous family, and how fortunate I had been to receive their kindness.

I spoke of how they had saved the Weabonga school, telling them of my plans to leave after just one term if matters didn't improve for me. They were surprised, as they hadn't realised until then the depth of my stress or the importance of their intervention. They said they'd just responded to a young man's obvious need for better living conditions. This was a revelation to me—I hadn't realised my distress was so obvious.

When we parted the next morning, we didn't hug. Men didn't then. But we exchanged deeply meant farewells.

So, the day after the concert I drove up the hill out of Weabonga for the last time, waving to the mothers and children who were out and about.

My darling friends Perc and Ethel waited out on the side of the road to make me stop and give them both a kiss in parting. I never saw either of them again.

Epilogue

Life after Weabonga quickly became crowded and rushed. The following year, 1962, I started teaching at a new school, married in August, commenced a university education—as a part-time, evening student—and found and settled into a new home. We all shivered as the threat of nuclear war loomed large and gave thanks when JFK and Khrushchev were able to reach agreement over Cuba.

During 1963 I commenced working as a casual bookie's clerk, every Saturday at the racetrack for the Waterhouse bookmaker brothers, as well as running the large drive-in bottle department as a casual manager at the Waterhouse family's Bronte Charles Hotel. I'd found that a teacher's wage was incapable of supplying all that a young family needed.

Our son was also born that year.

Life was hectic—teaching, studying, pencilling at the track, running the bottle-oh, and parenting. Time was a precious commodity. Keeping in touch with the good people of Weabonga was difficult, dwindled and eventually came to a halt.

I had learnt some news, though, from my infrequent contacts: Perc and Ethel had deteriorated in health quite dramatically soon after our parting. Medical advice was for them to be moved into a nursing home in Tamworth in early 1962. They lasted there only a few months, both dying within a short time. On receiving this news I reflected that their having to leave their beloved, though challenging, surrounds had been an error—too great a shock. But what else was to happen to two old people needing care? I grieved I hadn't seen them and missed them terribly.

Paul informed me of his upcoming marriage, although I was unable to travel to Tamworth to celebrate with him.

The Weabonga school closed in 1968 with the remaining small number of students travelling each day to the Niangala school.

I continued to believe in child-centred schooling. I accepted a role as educational adviser to a number of progressive schools, financed and run by parents, on Sydney's North Shore. My completed doctoral thesis was an in-depth evaluation of 'Open Education', the most serious attempt ever to implement a schooling system that promoted the child making many educational decisions.

My interest in Indigenous Australians also continued, and when I was awarded the Medal of the Order of Australia the citation read, in part, 'for contributions to education and educational research, and advocacy for Indigenous causes'.

~

In 2017 I was invited to a reunion of the students from Balmain Teachers College who had completed their training in 1957—sixty years before. One result of that get-together was a suggestion that the men who had one-teacher school experience record their thoughts, mostly for historical interest. I agreed to contribute a few thousand words. But once I'd begun, all the memories, which I'd thought would be meagre, came flooding back and I had much to record.

My son, on seeing the growing manuscript, urged me to write as much as I found interest in doing. So, like Topsy a bit, the story grew and grew.

With many thousands of words written, as I sat composing at my desk one day, I heard Perc speaking. I hadn't heard him for fifty-seven years, and he'd been dead for fifty-six, but I had no doubt it was his voice: that deep, mellifluous and lilting voice, slightly rural in tone and timbre, but clipped, no slow country drawl. Perc suggested that my manuscript be published so that he and Ethel would become known to more people. How extraordinary. Perc, in life, had asked nothing for himself, and now, from the grave, was whispering about immortality. He and Ethel remained alive in my mind, and perhaps I was the only one still with memories of them.

After not visiting Weabonga for fifty-seven years, I returned at my son's urging in July 2019.

The day I returned I learned that only one of my 1961 pupils remained in the village. In the story I called that student Mark Thomas. I found him living in the Thomas family home in the village.

Mark recognised me. 'I remember you,' he said. 'You were the teacher who had that little brown-and-cream car. That small square, boxy one.'

'That's right,' I confirmed, 'how remarkable of you, Mark, to remember that after all this time.'

He said he was now seventy years old and had spent his entire working life in the Australian Army. He had served in Vietnam, as had the two Mason boys, Jack and Steve. I was appalled by this news. As I listened, my thoughts were racing. *I didn't work to support, sustain and enable these kids to have their marble pulled out in a lottery of death. How could our nation have done that to three such wonderful boys? Indeed, how could our nation have done that to anyone's kids?*

But Mark told me that he, at least, had been a volunteer, not a conscript. He said he couldn't wait to enrol in the army.

'Oh no! I would have thought that the wrong career choice for you,' I couldn't help blurting out. To me, he was still the interesting youngster from 1961 with a rich inner life, aware of and sensitive to ideas and people. I thought the army might demand other qualities and best reward those who were more easily and happily resigned to a life controlled and ordered for them. I had never viewed Mark in that way.

However, I was reassured he had loved his military life and had, in a way, married the army, having never partnered or helped to raise a family. He lived now on his own.

Mark told us that, in his opinion, all the children from 1961 had lived successful lives. He proffered news of some.

Three O'Callaghans, Tom, Mike and Phil, had all become landholders in their own right. I was delighted to hear that news, as I had always hoped that Tom, in particular, had achieved his heartfelt wish.

Mark added that the youngest O'Callaghan, Charlie, now owned a fleet of trucks in a thriving transport business in Tamworth. Jill's three sons had built her a new home on a plot next to the old, decrepit wooden house, after Lawrie had died. Mark said that Jill, as far as he knew, had been very happy there until her death.

Joe and Jimmy Wallace had been selected to attend Farrer High, gone on to university and graduated as engineers.

Mark's sisters had married happily, although Vickie had no children.

After saying goodbye to Mark, my son and I called in to the Williamson homestead and were received graciously by Paul's son, an impressive chap in his thirties. We were told Paul had a family of five, extended the home to better accommodate them all, constructed a tennis court for the children's pleasure, and had been a well-loved dad. He had also contributed to the community by being elected as a shire councillor, a role he toiled at for many years.

The day we visited, Paul's son was preparing to drive into Tamworth to assist on the sidelines of the Tamworth Pirates rugby game scheduled for that afternoon. Like his father, he loved rugby and, while no longer an active player, was happy to help out in the club that his father had helped establish.

He explained the origin of the Pirates. I had been concerned by the influence of those I labelled 'born to rule' in the affairs of the Tamworth Rugby Club, and I now heard that tensions created by them had come to a head in 1962. Paul and a number of other young graziers and farm lads, disenchanted by the disputes in the club, had split and formed a new team: the Pirates.

Paul's son said his dad and others were totally put off by the 'toffee noses'. My response was to welcome and support Paul's decision of 1962, and to explain to the son what Paul and I had experienced from the 'born to rule' crowd. I understood well what Paul had taken exception to and what had forced his hand—though it wouldn't have been easy to quit a club of which he and I had enjoyed being part. His son said the new outfit attracted a strong following from among tradesmen, a group I'd never met in the 1960 Tamworth rugby scene, and the Pirates were immediately successful. *Well done, Paul*, I thought.

We heard that Paul had died about eighteen years earlier, aged about sixty-five or so, when he suffered a fall while working on his own in an outlying paddock. He hadn't been found until it was too late. That news shook me a little, redolent as it was of the fatal accident suffered by his mother.

Passing to and from the Williamson property, my son and I drove several times over the Swamp Oak Creek and alongside it for a stretch. It was dry: the bed was just dust and rocks and boulders. Such obvious evidence of drought was disturbing to me. In 1960 and 1961 the creek was in perpetual flow.

On visiting the site of Perc and Ethel's dwellings, we found only Ethel's small wooden cabin left standing. A willy-willy had destroyed the other two corrugated-iron huts in their entirety. Wires now hooked Ethel's cabin to the power pole outside the property. What a relief that electricity would have been to the two of them when living there.

Just standing on their home site filled me with peaceful memories, and I gave thanks, once more, for their appearance in my life when I'd been a desperate and stressed young man. As I looked around, I thought that only my immediate family had been more important to me in life than the two of them. How I had loved them.

The village looked different in quite a few ways. It took me a while to realise the Catholic chapel and the home that had run the post office from its veranda were no longer standing: fire had destroyed them both. Strewn around the two sites were abandoned cars, trucks, buses, utes.

The community hall, on the corner above the PO, remained standing, looking more spruce and solid than it ever had in my time. However, white ants had bored into the wooden foundations. The building was unstable, its use forbidden by the shire council. There was no plan to restore the footings, so it had reached the end of its life.

The school building was almost exactly as it had been sixty years earlier, despite not having been used as a school for more than fifty. After being granted a heritage listing, it has been preserved, now occupied as a home. The resident owner invited us in so that I could revisit the space. While I was chuffed by the heritage caveat, the owner was chagrined by his inability to add a back veranda: the shape of the little building had to be preserved. The owner had installed a huge wide-screen TV, satellite dish on the roof, running water, a solar boiler, mains electricity, and a landline phone. A laptop computer and a mobile phone were obvious. The storeroom was now a fully functioning bathroom and a fully equipped kitchen was installed on the veranda, which was built in some time after I'd left. How exhilarated the children and I would have been if we'd had just some of that technology and facilities way back in 1960. What might we have done together?

I found the schoolroom had been converted into a comfortable bedsitter, but the elements were still all around me, the shape and space were intact, and it was easy and moving to set all the children in place once more and think of the joyful and productive times we had spent there.

I reminisced that in our one-room bush school, the children and I had been happy, and known what had been achieved, where we needed to go and where we wanted to be. We encouraged and adopted any student suggestion and planned for spontaneity, giving space and time to promote it. We followed up individual interests as thoroughly as we could, although we were hampered by our limited materials. Our small school setting determined that individualised programs were necessary, and we achieved much on a personalised basis. Each child's reading and maths programs had all been left behind on my leaving the school on flashcards in the bank of shoeboxes in the storeroom.

On that day in July, as I stood reflecting, I came to believe that the Weabonga children and I had created a genuinely successful learning environment. The bush school was what we wanted it to be. No doubt we might have done more these days—with the technology available in the room as it was now, we could have been even more successful and better able to be child centred.

Standing there with the ghosts of the children swirling around me, I thought that education today should look forward to and embrace the outstanding benefits that technology is bringing and will yet bring to all children. Technology, I hoped, would open education for all.

I felt more positive and hopeful about the realisation of child-focused and centred education than I had ever been. Bring on individualised, responsive programs, and bring on open and progressive education, I thought—children will be happy and prosper. I felt certain, though, that even with increased use of the best forms and types of technology, teachers would never be replaced.

Internally, I recited a set of beliefs I had formed with the help of the children whose shapes were present all around me.

Good teachers model the best human behaviours of kindness, inclusion, sensitive encouragement and caring. They respond to kids by sustaining, enabling and valuing each child to ensure they can enjoy being who they are, love the life they lead and embrace whom they might become. Children need human contact, human support and guidance, and human affirmation. Teachers are indispensable and always will be.

Our Weabonga children of 1960 and 1961, in our bush school, helped me understand that. I salute them.

Acknowledgements

Many assisted in the telling of this story and I acknowledge and thank them all.

Patricia has never visited Weabonga but she retains memories of our chats and my letters about the village and school from 1960 and 1961. Her reminders illuminated much of the writing.

Sean, my son, when he saw the growing manuscript, suggested it might make a fine subject for a television documentary or filmed recreation, so I pushed ahead. Sean also urged me to revisit Weabonga recently, accompanied me, and captured a wonderful set of photographs.

During that visit we were hosted in the old school, the Williamson property, and the Thomas property. That kindness and generosity were important to me and I am grateful for them.

At times I needed to check my memory of Tamworth and went immediately to its wonderful history *City on the Peel: A History of Tamworth and District 1818–1976*, written by my dear friend Roger Milliss.

Judy Nunn and Bruce Venables encouraged my writing and suggested ways of approaching topics and dialogue. Their support and wisdom had me joking about their having created 'The Bays Literary Institute'.

But special acknowledgement and thanks must go to the wonderful team at Allen & Unwin. Jane Palfreyman immediately saw the possibilities in the first draft and shepherded the enterprise throughout. Kate Goldsworthy and Samantha Kent assisted so brilliantly through their careful editing and sensitive suggestions. Thank you also to cover designer Christa Moffitt and map-designer Mika Tabata.

Author Peter O'Brien and some of his original 1960/61 students, enjoying a reunion at the schoolhouse in Weabonga, November 2020.
PHOTOGRAPH: SEAN O'BRIEN